Small Business
Breakthrough

Small Business Breakthrough

John Blake
Joanna Buckingham
Ged Fish
Geoffrey Gregory
Charles Harvie
Peter Lawrence (editor)
Chris McEvoy
Richard Mole
John Whittaker

Loughborough University Small Business Unit

Department of Management Studies

Basil Blackwell

© Peter Lawrence 1985

First published 1985

Basil Blackwell Ltd
108 Cowley Road, Oxford OX4 1JF, UK

Basil Blackwell Inc.
432 Park Avenue South, Suite 1505,
New York, NY 10016, USA

British Library Cataloguing in Publication Data

Small business breakthrough.
   1. Small business—Great Britain—Case studies
   I. Blake, John
   338.6′42′0722   HD2346.G7
   ISBN 0–631–14407–2

Library of Congress Cataloging in Publication Data
Main entry under title:

Small business breakthrough.

   Bibliography: p.
   Includes index.
   1. Small business—Great Britain—Management.
   2. Small business—Great Britain—Management—Case
studies.   I. Blake, John (John D.)   II. Lawrence, Peter (Peter
A.)   III. Loughborough University of Technology. Small Business Unit.
HD62.7.S58   1985   658′.022′0941   85–8908
ISBN 0–631–14407–2

Typeset by Oxford Publishing Services, Oxford
Printed in Great Britain by Billing & Sons, Worcester

Contents

Acknowledgements

Our chief thanks go to the eleven companies at the centre of this book. They have been variously visited and studied, interviewed and discussed, indeed generally 'worked over', and have submitted to it all with good grace. We thank them and wish them well.

Three final-year students at the University of Loughborough have contributed indirectly to the book, in that each wrote a dissertation on one of the eleven companies, under the guidance of one of the authors. We would like to thank these students, now graduates – Karen Lowe, Nino Pucacco and Henry Rosoe.

Lastly, we would like to thank our secretaries in the Management Studies Department at Loughborough University for typing the manuscript at various stages. Our thanks are due to Marion Aitkenhead, Lesley Duckitt, Olivia Fergus, Kathleen Gibson, Aeron Hall, Margaret McMillan, Yvonne Marshall and Lisa Thirlby.

Preface

This book is the product of an ambition and an opportunity. The ambition was to write a book that was directly about small businesses, especially in the critical phase of the start-up and the early years. The opportunity was provided by the series of MIDAS (Melton Industrial Development Aid Scheme) business competitions in Leicestershire.

Since 1982, various local authorities together with Pedigree Petfoods of Melton Mowbray have mounted a yearly business competition where would-be entrepreneurs with ideas for a new business, or small businesses seeking to expand, compete for prize packages of venture capital money, facilitated favourable interest loans, assisted premises and consultancy support. The Small Business Unit at Loughborough University has been involved in these competitions, variously vetting applications, interviewing entrants and doing some research on the operation.

In its second year, 1983, the MIDAS competition was supported by Leicestershire County Council, Leicester City Council, Pedigree Petfoods and Leicestershire Business Venture. Entrants came from all over Britain but winners were required to move into the area. There were ten winners.

Our idea was to see what happened afterwards. So we followed up eight out of these ten winners for a year and a half after the competition, together with three other companies we got to know at this time and which seemed at an interesting stage of development. This group of eleven small businesses stands at the centre of this book. We are in a certain way telling their story, sometimes individually, sometimes in terms of generalizations.

At the same time we have taken ideas from other sources as well – from reading and discussion, but particularly from former and wider experience of small firms. Most of the authors have earlier experience of, and interest in, small firms and this has generated some of the ideas developed here and provided many of the illustrative examples introduced in the text.

There are three natural readerships for this book. First, there are a growing number of students, including undergraduates, on small business courses; this book is a contribution to the literature they draw on. Second, there are also a growing number of people involved in helping and advising small firms – accountants, solicitors, counsellors representing various government organizations, local government officers, and, occasionally, business consultants. They have a use for lifelike accounts of the small business reality. Third, there are the practitioners, and would-be practitioners. The owners and managers of small firms know much of what is in this book from experience, but they may still get some fun from seeing a mirror held up to their world; while those thinking of taking the creative and intimidating step of founding their own business may take both warning and inspiration from these pages.

Peter Lawrence
Melton Mowbray

1 The Real World of the Small Businessman

The Cat vanished. Alice was not much surprised at this, she was getting used to queer things happening. While she was looking at the place where it had been, it suddenly appeared again.

(Lewis Carroll, *Alice in Wonderland*)

One of the companies that figures in this book, Light Fantastic, has a holographic gallery on the south side of the redeveloped Covent Garden site in London. A centrepiece of the main room is a holographic representation of the Cheshire Cat: it is there, not there, or only partly there depending on the angle at which you look at it.

Small business is like this. What the outsider looking in and trying to understand sees depends a lot on the angle, and it matters to get this angle right. In particular it is not very helpful to assume that small businesses are like big companies but on a smaller scale. Indeed the big firm analogy really obscures a good deal, since small businesses are qualitatively different and inhabit a differently structured environment.

This difference consists in part of uncertainty, especially in the start-up phase, and often an element of living from hand to mouth, small firms being much more directly impinged on by an often hostile environment. By the same token, the small firm owner–manager is sometimes able to take direct initiatives and have a one-man effect on immediate events. It is themes of this kind that we illustrate in this first chapter.

Cosy Chaos

One of the ironies of advanced industrial society is that a relatively small proportion of the labour force, not much more than a quarter in Britain, actually work in manufacturing industry. In other words, there are more people out there looking in than there are objects of study! This is probably a root cause of the general public's various misapprehensions about industry, of which the most prevalent is the conviction that industry is orderly, organized and rational.

The departures from this rational model – the crises, disruptions, breakdowns, stockouts, and threatened strikes – are all too familiar to the insider, as are the imponderables, the 'guestimates', cover-ups and inspired snatching of chestnuts from fires. Yet big companies can usually present a semblance of order. They have resources, structure and hierarchy, sometimes company rules and job descriptions and they are buffered from the environment in various ways. Small firms, on the other hand, are often studies in a cosy state of chaos.

Consider as an illustration the following excerpts from the preliminary visit notes of one of the team to a 'widget' factory in the south-west. The company concerned is small, traditional and has been handed down from father to son for 100 years. At the time of the visit, the company was run by the father, in his fifties, watched with moody resentment by the eldest son, in his twenties. The father's cousin ran a rival firm, equally small, nearby. The following impressions found their way into the visit notes:

> The machinery varies from old to ancient. There are many different presses with different tonnage pressures. I cannot imagine that these are ever all going at the same time, but maybe they are in the morning when the father gets in retired people who want to earn a little extra money. It is very manual, pulling down levers to press each sheet individually. There are even two machines at the back and down some very rickety stairs where the worker pulls on a rope to release the top weight to press the sheet. This machine has to press each

sheet twice! As each widget is made up of two sheets, this equals four pressings for each widget. The man who was showing me round the factory explained that he had done it for about an hour and gained very severe blisters. The man operating the machine seemed as old as it was, and deaf from the noise it made. The dyes have a tendency to crack. As each costs a lot (*c*.£500) it pays to repair them as best you can. I was shown how a little bit of water in the mould helped with the pressing – they did not know why, it just did!

The factory layout is bizarre. There are three floors, with machines haphazardly arranged – the processes waste a lot of time in having to carry everything upstairs for one process and then back down again for another. I found out later this was literally due to the fact that when a new machine was bought it went where there was room. This was often simply the place it was left when delivered. Often machinery was collected from big widget producers who were getting rid of archaic machinery. These acquisitions were sometimes for stripping to use the parts as spares, and also sometimes simply to stop rivals getting hold of the machines. In consequence there was a lot of partially working machinery taking up floor space.

The women worked upstairs tying together the two halves of the widget. They all seemed happy, a family firm atmosphere, though I think the pay was very poor. The newest recruits (women – all the men seemed old) were downstairs loading a Heath Robinson type machine, home-made and it looked like it.

And again:

The company suffers the problems of all satellite companies. Completely at the mercy of the big widget makers, who could demand that an order could be turned out on a very tight schedule.

The father/boss is always on the shop floor, lending a hand with all the different processes. He is very anti-change and has a sort of 'serf' approach to the 'lords' – in this case the big widget manufacturers. They all owe him money, but he sees this as a safety net.

He did not seem to have any system of invoices and receipts; the office consisted of a battered chair, a telephone and out of date directory. There was no computer.

The idea of rearranging the factory he sees as completely out of the question – it would mean closing, possibly for a week.

When there is a delivery of sheets of steel ('the steel's getting thinner, the quality is not what it was'), the lane outside is completely blocked. So everybody in the factory stops and rushes out to offload the lorry.

Delegation to the son is completely 'out of order'. He is treated as another worker and is not privy to his father's decisions. As decisions/deals are never written down in an obvious way the son is effectively excluded; this does not help their relationship. The business is completely dependent on the father who knows everything about everything. He has to strip down machinery and find out what is wrong, deal with customers, fight his cousin and keep his head above water. He is very paternalistic with his staff.

We have quoted at length from this case not so much because it is extreme, but rather illustrative of many features that characterize many small companies. True, many small firms, certainly those that get publicity, embody modern technologies and an increasing number of, especially new, small firms find themselves in attractive and convenient premises on industrial estates. Yet there are many still in ramshackle buildings, embodying every operating illogicality. The hostility to change, the unwillingness to step aside and get organized, the patchwork development of facilities are all too common. So is the lack of systems, even simple accounting and invoicing methods. Note, too, in the quoted example the absence of anything written: all is done on nods and winks, handshake deals, things the boss keeps in his head.

The father–son tension masks another reality, which is that the small firm generally lacks a management team. There is an owner–manager and there are worker–employees. The owner typically exercises all the management functions (they do not all have sons, or trust them) and works on the shop floor when needed. He is his own repairman, fixer and maintenance fitter.

Life Is Not in Straight Lines

There is another peculiarity of small businesses, which is connected with this lack of a management team even if it is not wholly explained by it. This is that accounts of small firms – what they are doing, how they got where they are etc. – are often surprisingly complicated, and curiously more complicated than the stories of big companies. There are several reasons for this. To try to make some of them clear, let us start with big companies.

A big company has a past, often a substantial past, and the general expectation is that it has a future too. Its identity is bound up with this dimension of elapsed and enduring time: or more simply, the passage of time makes possible an ordering of events, a positing of linkages, a perception of causes and connections. When big company executives, and for that matter corporate biographers, do this, when they so order, link and point to causes, they may be deceiving themselves or others. They may, that is, be engaging in 'post factum rationalization', in the construction of politically acceptable accounts, or in pure corporate cosmetics. The point is, however, that it is possible to do this, and the accounts usually have some verisimilitude.

There is another angle, which is that companies exist in space as well as time, and big companies fill more of it. Because big companies are big, they offer the possibility of seeing the big picture. Suppose you are chairman of ICI and one day, due to a failure in the management information system, you find out that the company employs a thieving foreman at one of its branches. You actually have the luxury of knowing that this is not important. The size of the company and its operations provide a yardstick for determining the importance of events.

It is not entirely a matter of size in a simple and direct way, however. It is also that big companies have functional specialization and hierarchical screening. Functional specialization. means essentially that the issues that come before a manager are determined by his department or function: he is an R & D (research and development) manager, so he deals with R & D questions; or he is area sales manager so he has salesmen reporting to him, not research scientists and so on. The issues are also screened in terms of triviality versus importance, the higher the manager the more exclusive his concern with serious issues. Only the general managers are concerned with the large general questions, which transcend the interests of the various separate functions, R & D, sales, engineering and so on.

The above is all elementary stuff but the critical point is that none of it applies to small firms: they often have no past, sometimes no future, no big picture, no functional specialization or hierarchical screening, no grading of issues to different levels of management. In short, no organizationally contrived way of seeing the wood for the trees.

This makes studying small businesses more difficult. There are seldom any written records – not only no corporate biographies, but little in the way of minutes and memos, reports or policy statements. One cannot tap specialist sources in the sense of going to the personnel department for an exposé of personnel policy, or talking to sales about pricing policy. Neither can one 'go to the top' as a court of last appeal for the elucidation of critical issues. In the small company the top is the only place there is.

We have introduced these ideas because we believe they are true and helpful to an understanding of small firms, but also because they explain things described in this book: concern with small events that turn out to be important, with chance, with good and bad fortune, and with complicated, messy stories of the struggles of small companies.

Changing Premises: a Traumatic Move

Small firms that are new tend to move; to change premises. The business often starts in a private house, garage or shed, and moves into industrial or commercial premises when the entrepreneur gives up paid employment to run his business full time. What is more, changes of premises are common in the early years: the entrepreneur wants a site that is bigger or cheaper, or less subject to some critical restriction, or something he can buy rather than rent, or whatever. Moreover entrepreneurs who win business competitions, which means most of the companies that figure in this book, are faced with a more or less obligatory move. Business competitions, paradoxically, do not have the primary objective of helping businesses develop but of providing employment in the locality of the sponsor–organizers. Thus winners are either obliged to move into the area, or if already there, find themselves making a local move because occupancy of a new unit, typically with a rent and rates 'holiday', is part of the winner's package.

On the face of it moves of this kind are a good idea. They are typically into new accommodation, often free or at least subsidized in the first instance. In practice, however, these moves are seldom accomplished without some aggravation and on occasion can be disastrous. The company described in chapter 5 is a good example: the premises to which the prize-winning entrepreneur moved were too big, and therefore difficult to heat, too far away from home and functionally unsuitable (a former cattle-food store to be used for the manufacture of precision optical instruments).

This is the worst example in a sample of a dozen or so companies, yet others too had problems. One initially sad case concerns a company, again one of the prize-winners in the business competition, which was moving from cramped and inadequate premises in south London to an industrial unit on a new estate in the Midlands. In this instance the partners running the company were looking forward to the move and viewing the new premises as likely to be a change for the better. The contractor concerned gave a quotation and a completion date for the fitting out of the unit, but in the event this date came and went without anything happening. The partners then employed a local builder to do the fitting out, but this hiccup meant the company ceased trading for two months. This in turn meant not only a loss of revenue but a pressurizing backlog of orders when then company was able to resume production.

More was to come. The same company arrived on the new site with no telephone and were quoted a lead time in months for the connection by British Telecom. The company's small delivery van was vandalized in the early days and written off, and they discovered there were no collective security arrangements on the industrial estate. They now have their own guard dogs. This leads to another recurrent theme in the life of small firms – the relationship between the companies and their local authorities.

Local Government: Help or Hindrance?

The rational assumption would be that local authorities would welcome small firms within the area, and do their all to facilitate their success. Moreover, if these small firms were business competition winners, and the authorities themselves partners in the sponsorship, one would expect their commitment to the success of the local entrepreneurs to be redoubled. Not so: this rational view rests on two misapprehensions.

The first is that local authorities actually want industry. They do not. What they want is employment and rate revenue, and if there were a way of getting these without having manufacturing industry, they would find this infinitely preferable.

The second misapprehension is that the two sides have something in common; that they are working for the same ends. They are not; indeed they are working on different models. Local government administration is about probity, regulation, applying the rules and procedures, preventing infractions and derelictions and saving money. Its actions are constrained by accountability. Business is about chances, opportunities, cutting corners and making money. It is constrained by the need to get things done.

So perhaps it is not surprising that tension does arise between people running small firms and local government officers. Looking at it from the side of the companies, we discover charges of premises being unsuitable, or too dear, or rent rises too frequent; complaints about lack of security on industrial estates; failure of local authorities to provide amenities such as refuse collection, as well as occasional irritation by entrepreneurs at being 'told off' whenever they left a rubbish skip outside their unit or parked a truck there, or performed some other bylaw-violating act in the pursuance of the business.

Consider the following as an instance of the mentality and operating differences between small business and local authority. One of the companies was entitled to a local authority grant for money the company had spent on equipping a factory unit (heating appliances and other fixtures), the rationale being that the factory was only rented from the local authority and the building and fixtures would revert to the authority on the termination of the lease. The owner of the company intended to use this grant, £5,000, to cover the rates of £1,200 he owed to the same local authority. Only part of the grant was paid on time, the entrepreneur could thus not cover the rates and the authority promptly threatened to take him to court for non-payment.

No doubt there is a rational explanation – rates and grants are handled by different departments. This again leads to another recurrent theme in the life of the small businessman, the need for cash, and now.

My Kingdom For an Open Cheque

Many small businesses, especially in the start-up phase, have an acute need for ready money, and this conditions a lot of the things they do and things they do not do.

The need arises from several causes. First, money is normally needed to start a business – for premises, plant, equipment, goodwill and stock. Second, it is normal for a portion of this money to be borrowed, which means the recurrent burden of repayments. Third, the business needs working capital to buy materials and perhaps pay staff wages. (This working capital notion is presented more elegantly in chapter 7, where both its implications and ways of trying to do without it are examined.) Fourth, as the business starts up, or begins to expand after a plateau period, the initial effect is to push up the need for working capital. Payment for goods delivered or services rendered comes later. Again the effects of expansion and the concomitant danger of what is called overtrading are taken up in more detail in chapter 7, but these considerations are introduced here, briefly, to set the scene.

In short, the effect of all these factors is to put a lot of pressure on small, and especially new, business to generate revenue in the short run and to keep on doing it. This precarious balance between often tenuous revenue and recurrent commitments is easily upset. As one of our entrepreneurs put it, 'It doesn't take a lot to give us a problem.'

These constraints cause operators of small firms to do all sorts of things for the sake of cash now. One small company owner did all the delivery himself, although the firm employed blue collar staff, simply in the hope of getting paid on the spot. The big event was the trip to London: 'I try to do five drops in London and hope for two and a half grand – sometimes I end up with thirty quid.'

A common thread is that small companies do things that are not really in their longer term interests in order to get money in. Again, one of our companies selling to retailers used a middleman for one geographic sales area, the major point in the operation being that this middleman would guarantee a cheque within 14 days, while allowing the retailers to whom he on-sold 30 days' credit. The company got revenue quicker, but with profit margins lowered. Debt factoring has a similar effect. This method was also used by companies in our sample; it gives them money up front, but reduces margins.

It is only fair to add that one of our companies turned this money–time game to its advantage and got started in business by factoring on trade credit. This company bought in quantity from large manufacturers on 30 days' credit, reselling much of the stock in smaller lots for cash before its own payments were due. Another of our companies, fairly secure in its fourth year of trading, similarly turned the needs of others to its advantage, ringing round all its suppliers towards the end of any month when it had money to spare and asking for discounts for cash.

If sacrificing middle term margins to short term revenue is

a sort of 'sin of commission' that small companies engage in, some of the 'sins of omission' are worse. The most heart-rending case in the present study concerned a company that was offered a substantial export order by an up-market foreign retail chain and turned it down because they could afford neither the raw materials to manufacture the order nor the wait for eventual payment.

This need for ready money is the key to a further and related feature of the world of the small businessman, vulnerability.

Naked Among Wolves

Small firms do not typically have very much in reserve. Most or all of their eggs are in one basket – managerial talent is often restricted to a single owner–manager and if they owe the bank £8,000 it is their problem, whereas if they owed the bank £2 million it would be the bank's problem. So when things go wrong, they go badly wrong; or perhaps the critical thing is that what might otherwise be considered quite small blows have a magnified effect on smaller companiies, and our sample offered plenty of illustrations.

One of our companies, for example, was concerned to meet its VAT payment obligations but was advised by the accountant that the volume of business was too small for the company to be liable (that is, under £13,000 a year). Then the company got some special and very lucrative orders a little outside its basic operations and invoiced £4,000 of completed work in ten days. It became liable for VAT for the period and had to pay the government what was due, but without having charged its customers VAT on the produce sold in the first place. This did not cripple the company, but it was a blow.

Another of our companies was running a small manu-facturing operation over a shop, its own retail outlet, but more importantly was engaged in a quite successful mail order business, with the bulk of the clients in Scotland and the north of England. The products were in the semi-luxury consumer goods category, the demand for which proved horribly elastic. In fact, the 1980 steel strike led to such a fall-off in the mail order business that the company was temporarily finished off and forced to close its shop.

Another company, described in more detail in chapter 5, had one supplier for an indispensable component and one major industrial customer for the output. Quite out of the blue the supplier announced a significant price rise, the major customer refused to accept a corresponding rise in the price of the finished product and the company suffered a blow from which it never quite recovered. The same company received another setback when its only agent was seduced away by a rival, leaving the company with no link to its end-user market.

These two misfortunes illuminate very well the vulnerability of many small companies. Take the first problem, the price rise demanded by a sole supplier. The solution is easy, a matter of pure common sense – get another supplier, or better still have two or more suppliers before the event and then none of them will dare to try on draconian price increases.

But there is a snag. There is absolutely no competition to supply small firms. Their orders are trivial in size and value, they are not especially good payers and they may not even be around in a year's time. Nor can the small firm's owner–manager pass the problem on to the purchasing department as an assignment to locate and sign up an alternative supplier for component X, because there is no purchasing department. Indeed, in this example it is a one-man firm, in which the owner himself does the product development and testing, the manufacturing, the buying and selling and the chasing after working capital and development funds. It is the same story with agents. Agents want to represent big successful companies with well-tried products, but who wants to be an agent for a one-man firm?

In another of our partnership companies while the owners were renovating a newly acquired property as a new site for production, they delegated day to day responsibilities to their superviser. The latter, however, abused his position of trust and both stole some of the high quality raw material and substitued some lower quality material for it, thereby causing substandard goods to be dispatched. The fraud was discovered, of course, and the superviser dismissed, but as a result of the raw material loss and need to investigate the company lost two weeks' production, as well as having a restitution problem with some of its customers.

One of the companies which won a prize in the business competition had trouble with its accountants, from whom it had taken advice before entering the competition. The accountants had offered to prepare supporting document-ation for the company's entry on a sliding scale fee basis. If, that is, the company won the high value first prize, they would pay the accountants a high fee; if the entry resulted in a lower value award, they would pay a correspondingly lower fee. The company entered and was placed, but without coming first: the accountants invoiced them for the higher fee and refused to release the accounts until it was paid.

Again these two tales show something of the plight of the small company when misfortune strikes. Light-fingered foremen and unethical accountants are hopefully a rarity from everyone's point of view, but a big company can withstand these setbacks. For the first of these companies, however, the dishonest foreman was the only foreman they had, so they lost intermediate supervision as well as money. The second company had its disagreement with the accoun-tant at a time when it had moved to new premises and was experiencing a variety of other teething problems.

Perils of the Export Trip

In trying to depict the world of the small business we have referred both implicitly and explicitly to the standards and practices of big companies to set off the reality of small business. To round off the contrast, an example of a different kind may be helpful. First, let us set the scene by noting big company practice in the field of export.

When a company based in Brtain sends one of its export managers on a trip abroad there is a common activity and intent. Most often the manager is going to visit existing customers in the foreign territory rather than search for new ones. In marketing language, the trip is more likely to be about 're-order' selling than 'missionary' selling. What is more, the manager is unlikely to go out cold. Someone will have made bookings and reservations for him, and planned an itinerary. More often than not the export manager goes to see the company's agent or agents in the country concerned, and the agent will arrange meetings with customers, actual or potential, mediate and even interpret if necessary. The agent, indeed, will probably arrange a local itinerary, decide whom the manager will meet and when, and brief him beforehand. And of course, the manager does not actually take a consignment of the company's products with him (truck drivers and freight agents do this), though he may of course take samples and will certainly have literature on the company's product range.

Although small, several of our companies were selling abroad, and in one case the owner describe for us his first export trip to Belgium. It is an instructive tale.

The owner loaded up his van with £1,500 worth of produce and drove on to the boat. On the way over he checked the currency rate at the purser's office to know what price to charge for items in Belgian francs.

On arrival at Ostend it emerged that the Belgian customs were on strike. He was asked no questions about the van and its load, given no opportunity to make declarations or pay VAT. There was just a desultory passport check.

It should be said at this point that our entrepreneur has no fixed plan. He has no existing customers in Belgium, no agent, no contacts, no list of useful addresses for cold-calling. Instead he cruised the streets of Antwerp simply looking for retailers who would be interested in what he had to sell, and indeed he got lucky. He met one retailer who said he was definitely interested in doing business and even thinking of buying the whole consignment. He suggested they should have a further discussion after lunch, when the retailer's wife, who spoke better English, would be present. Our entrepreneur returned to his parked vehicle after lunch, and was arrested in the street on a smuggling charge.

A day of interrogation followed, at the end of which he was made to pay a cautionary fine of £1,500 but told he was now free to sell the produce. On release he resumed the interrupted dialogue with the retailer and sold him the whole consignment for £1,500, thereby averting disaster.

It may not always be as colourful as this on a selling trip, but these things do happen in the world of small business.

The aftermath is also revealing. The entrepreneur got more orders from the same retailer, which he was able to meet without hitch, securing the services of an agent at Ostend who arranged the documentation and saw to the VAT. Inquiries from other retailers in Belgium flooded in but, said the entrepreneur, 'it is not really worth going because the truck only holds £1,500 worth.' He much prefers a new customer from Holland with his own transport who picks up what he wants. It simply is one of the peculiarities of small business that small things determine big things.

The Entrepreneur is the Company

Purposefulness and imprinting are the obverse of vulnerability and risk in the world of small business. The entrepreneur is the company, even where there are employees and not just a working owner or working partners. The company rests on his ideas and inspiration. He has fashioned, developed or construed the products or conceived of a service to be offered; he is the organization, the style, the search for markets and the trading system.

All this makes small companies an interesting site for the study of business ideas. Whereas with large and established companies the basic idea is often obscured by diversification, history, size and structure, the small company encapsulates a business idea in simple, identifiable form. In our group, for example, one company has appreciated that holograms can be used for emblematic and representational purposes, and can thus be developed for advertising. Another company has developed two quite new accessory products for the leisure industry, while yet another is founded on the expectation of developing a sophisticated industrial product.

But the business ideas do not always embody newness on this scale. A leading firm in the group makes wind generators, which are not new at all, but the entrepreneur in question has developed a version that overcomes previous limitations with a great gain in efficiency and application. One business is based on the simple recognition of a gap between large manufacturers of a basic product and the need of many purchasers to buy it in customized and assembled lots. Another company derives from an understanding of how computers and programming resources can be utilized to develop a production-related service to industry. Yet another is making something that is not new at all but is exploiting superior design to reach the top end of the retail market, while another is making conventional products in a new material.

Two of our companies owe much of their success to being able to undercut American suppliers to UK markets, and one of them was formed quite explicitly to exploit this strategy. Our group also includes a management buy-out company which by definition is simply continuing (part of) the business of the former owners, but with the advantage of knowing the things the former owners did and did not do that brought them to the point of sale.

In other words, our quite small sample illustrates a range of business-entry, price and marketing strategies. We will take the theme further, first in the next chapter which looks at links between what the entrepreneurs did before starting their companies and the kind of business they have gone into, and also in Chapter 8 which looks at the question of the relationship between the small business and the market.

A byproduct of the smallness and informality of such businesses is that there is little in the way of personnel systems, or standardization of pay and conditions for employees. Most firms in our sample actually have employees but their reward and treatment of them is more variable than would be tolerated in larger established enterprises. Small firms are not generally good payers, and we identified some which clearly were not. We also have one whose operations are discussed particularly in chapters 7 and 8 where production was based entirely on a system of outworkers. One of the companies insisted on high piece-work performance rates (and was clearly getting rid of employees who could not make the grade) and another declined all sick pay for employees but found ways of rewarding well workers and supervisers deemed especially loyal. Another of the firms drew into its operations a student who was studying it, and after graduation he became their consultant.

The Element of Luck

According to their own testimonies, luck has played a larger part in the fortunes of these small businesses than it would for larger established firms, and in saying this we do not refer simply to hard luck stories. Many offer accounts of lucky breaks in the start-up period or at some other critical stage.

The proprietors of one of our companies described the benefits of having an article about their product range published in a magazine. This led to an invitation to the company to be represented at a trade exhibition which in turn led to in its winning an award for its designs from a national circulation magazine. This accolade so impressed the building society that it (at last) agreed to advance funds for the purchase of proper manufacturing premises, the company having previously used makeshift accommodation.

Another of our entrepreneurs was acutely aware of the importance of ready money in the early stage. Before launching out, this entrepreneur went to visit a firm abroad for whom he had once done subcontract work while a manager of another company, and where he had built up something of a personal relationship with the head. This firm had a major order for an institutional buyer in its own country and agreed to subcontract a specialist part of the operation to our entrepreneur. What is more, the foreign firm agreed to pay the entrepreneur immediately on delivery – £32,000. Of course, it might be argued that this is a little more than luck!

2 The Occupational Link

This chapter will introduce the eleven companies in the case sample, naming them and their location, describing what they make or what service they provide and who owns or runs them. Several of these companies will be the subjects of single chapters later in the book.

First, however, we will examine the connection between these entrepreneurs' previous occupational experience and the businesses they have in fact founded, and argue for a strong and positive connection. This information will also be viewed within the wider context of the debate about education and entrepreneurialism.

Education and the Supply of Entrepreneurs

The literature suggests that the supply of entrepreneurs is related to several factors, including social class, religious affiliation, education and position in the family.

These factors are very closely linked, however, so that it is rarely possible to identify any one as being the single most important variable. Education, however, is generally regarded as being one of the more important factors in contributing to the supply of entrepreneurs, and it figures significantly in the literature. While recognizing that other factors such as social class may have some relevance for the supply of entrepreneurs, we will concentrate here on education, defining it first in conventional academic terms, and then considering previous occupational experience as education.

Many commentators have noted that high academic qualifications are, in some industries, a necessary but never a sufficient condition for entrepreneurial success. That is, for some industries one may need a high formal qualification to get into the business at all, but having the qualification does not guarantee that the company one founds will do well. In a study of a large number of small companies, Storey,[1] for example, found no evidence to support the view that educationally qualified founders of companies are more likely to establish profitable firms, or to have a high level of turnover. What is more, the process of invention is often a lonely one, so that many inventors are fiercely independent, but at the same time poor communicators. The successful running of a business requires entrepreneurs to possess communicative and personal skills that are not necessarily associated with intellect.

The Benefits of a Good Formal Education

The presumptive advantages of formal education for the would-be entrepreneur, as canvassed in the relevant literature, are:

- he/she will have a greater choice both of his/her initial occupation, and of the industry in which he/she will work;
- he/she is more likely to have obtained some managerial experience prior to establishing his/her firm;
- he/she is more likely to have greater confidence to begin his/her enterprise;
- in the more sophisticated and technically advanced industries, micro electronics for instance, only those with the highest educational qualifications could consider establishing firms. These industries have often been associated with institutes of advanced education, such as universities.

These ideas on the link between entrepreneurs and their educational background are taken up in studies by Roberts and Wainer,[2] Nicholson and Brinkley[3] and Boswell.[4] It is interesting that Gudgin, Brunskill and Fothergill,[5] in a study of new manufacturing firms in the East Midlands, do show that firms founded and managed by people with degrees or equivalent qualifications perform significantly better than those founded by non-graduates. On the other hand, the authors do not discuss the role of inter-industry differences (that is, does the relationship hold for all types of industry or just the more technically sophisticated?), nor do they discuss the possibility that the results are slewed by a few extreme cases in a relatively small sample.

Again Storey[6] does find a positive relationship between educational qualifications and the performance of his firms in manufacturing but this relationship was found to be weak or non-existent for non-manufacturing companies. In other words, although there is an extensive literature on the relationship between formal education and entrepreneurialism it does not offer a great deal of hard evidence of a positive association between the two. Moreover, it is clear that any positive association that does exist relates to manufacturing industry not business in general, and there is a suspicion that the relationship derives from high technology branches of industry in particular.

The Occupational Background

Now we will broaden the notion of education as previously discussed to include not just education of a formal academic nature, but also that acquired from previous employment or business ownership experience. If we do this, we are making the notion of education more realistic, particularly so in the case of our sample of small businesses. The acquisition of skills and knowledge from previous employment or business ownership is another important educational source, which we can regard as being of a more practical nature. We call this phenomenon 'occupational linkage'.

The view that there is a strong link between an entrepreneur's occupational background and the business he creates fits in well with the discussion of the characteristics of new firm founders in the overall literature, from which the following propositions emerge:

- new firm founders may form their new business in the industries in which they were formerly employed (or in which they previously owned a business);
- a number of entrepreneurs begin their business on a part-time basis, which enables them to assess the ultimate viability of the enterprise;
- unemployment can act as a positive incentive to start a business;
- a new business could be created out of frustration with existing employment.

For our sample of firms, it is predominantly the first point which appears to be of most relevance.

Our Chosen Entrepreneurs

Now we will discuss in more detail the occupational (education, and business experience) backgrounds of the proprietors of the small businesses in our sample.

The small businesses featured in this book are predominantly past MIDAS award winners (see p.vii) and they are mostly situated in the East Midlands.

These companies are: Ensign Computers Limited (Leicester); Sycon Products Limited (Leicester); Optical Systems Limited (Draycott, near Derby); Euro Energy Resources Limited (Blaby, Leicestershire); Marlec Engineering Limited (Oakham, Leicestershire); Inhalation Therapy Products Limited (Market Harborough, Leicestershire); Pro Stock Glass Limited (Ashby-de-la-Zouch, Leicestershire); Light Fantastic (London); Victoria East Limited (Ashbourne, Derbyshire); Leather Fashions Limited (Manchester); Polstar Limited (Newcastle upon Tyne).

There are some general observations to be made about our sample of firms. It is clear that a strong link exists between the occupational (particularly previous employment or business ownership) background of the entrepreneurs and the businesses which they have created in 10 out of the 11 small businesses. Only in the case of Victoria East is there no obvious link. In this case the proprietor's natural flair for designing and her self-taught skills made it possible for her to start the business. What knowledge she has acquired from her previous employment has largely been on the managerial rather than product side.

Turning next to the educational background of our entrepreneurs, we find a noticeable lack of formal educational qualifications. The breakdown in regard to this is as follows:

Degrees	1
Diplomas/others	3
HNC/ONC	2
None	5

Of those in the none category, two did serve an apprenticeship.

If we now turn to the business management training of our sample, we observe the following breakdown:

Formal business management training	3
Limited business management training	2
No business management training	6

Hence, for our small sample of entrepreneurs, most had not obtained formal business management training. If, however we analyse our sample again, but this time for instances of previous practical business management experience, we obtain some interesting results:

From previous employment	6
From previous or existing business ownership	4
No previous business management experience	1

Here we have uncovered something quite striking. While the formal academic qualifications obtained by our entrepreneurs are not significant, particularly in the case of higher educational qualifications, taking the group as a whole, this is more than compensated for by the practical business experience they have gained.

From our sample of 11 small businesses, we notice that 10 of these have had some practical experience of business management, either from previous employment (6) or from the ownership of a previous or existing business (4). Only in one case, Pro Stock Glass, have the proprietors gained no previous business management experience, and have had to run their business very much on a learning-by-doing basis, though even in this case the two partners have a variety of useful and relevant work experience behind them (see table 2.7).

The Case Sample

The backgrounds of our sample of small businesses and of their proprietors are summarized in tables 2.1–2.11, and for the moment we merely seek to emphasize more precisely the particular occupational–product link for each case.

Ensign Computers Limited (table 2.1), produce computer programs to assist manufacturers with computerized systems. David Tillyard, who is one of the directors of the company, is responsible for the day-to-day running of the company. His own occupational background is a diverse

Table 2.1   Ensign Computers Limited

Proprietor	Mr D.J. Tillyard
Qualifications	
Degree	
Other	Diploma Management Studies; Diploma Institute of Works Management; Diploma Institute of Electrical and Electronic Engineers
Occupational experience	Technical trainee; trainee works manager; computer analyst and operations manager; administrative supervisor; salesman; sales manager
Previous experience of product	Gained from previous employment
Product	Computer programs to assist manufacturers with computerized systems
Business management experience	Both formal and practical. The practical element included that as sales manager, regional sales manager from previous employment and that obtained from being a director of Ensign Computers

one, and includes a strong managerial as well as computing component.

Sycon Products Limited (table 2.2) produce the Sycon tow bar steps and the Sycon trailer parker system. Bryan Roberts who runs the company has a long history of work in the motor trade. The diversification of his existing business, Roberts and Brooks (Syston) Limited, into new products and markets as a result of the recession hitting the motor trade led to the creation of a division known as Sycon Products. Roberts and Brooks had connections with camping and camping equipment, and they realized the potential for the products which Sycon is now developing and producing.

The linkage here is one from the declining motor trade sector into new but still vehicle-related areas of expansion. The existence of the original business helped to identify these new areas of expansion. Sycon Products is discussed in more detail in chapter 6.

Table 2.2   Sycon Products Limited

Proprietor	Mr B. Roberts

Qualifications
  Degree
  Other	

Occupational
  experience
	Motor manufacturer's apprenticeship;
	  involved in the development and
	  selling of exothermic heat treatment
	  kilns

Previous experience
  of product
	None, however the potential of such
	  products was obtained from the
	  parent company's involvement with
	  camping

Product	Sycon trailer parker system Sycon tow bar steps

Business
  management
  experience
	Acquired only through running
	  Roberts and Brooks (Syston) Limited,
	  of which Sycon Products is a division

Optical Systems Limited (table 2.3) design and develop a prototype range of optical coordinate measuring machines for industrial application. The firm's proprietor, Terry Corner, has acquired a wide range of skills during his previous employment, including some managerial experience. There

Table 2.3 Optical Systems Limited

Proprietor	Mr T.J. Corner

Qualifications
  Degree
  Other	

Occupational experience	Fitter; toolmaker; foreman; works engineer; manager of an optical instruments division, responsible for the production and development of machines for all types of industry in optics
Previous experience of product	Acquired from previous employment
Product	The design, development and manufacture of a prototype range of optical coordinate measuring machines for general industrial application
Business management experience	Gained from previous employment only

is a particularly strong link here between this entrepreneur's previous employment and his current business. Terry Corner has acquired significant experience in optics, which he is now applying in his own business. Optical Systems Limited is discussed in more detail in chapter 5.

Euro Energy Resources Limited (table 2.4) is in business to assemble specialist battery packs for the electronics industry and to package own-brand rechargeable batteries for a variety of users and outlets. The director, Roger Wilding, previously ran and still owns a retail/mail order model craft business, and this provided him with the relevant knowledge to create EER Limited. The connection is that his model business involved him in the purchase of batteries for use in conjunction with models sold from his shop. A clear link can be found in this case from previous business ownership experience, to the product which this new business is producing.

Marlec Engineering Limited (table 2.5), proprietor John Fawkes, manufacture wind generators for electrical fencing

Table 2.4   Euro Energy Resources Limited

Proprietor	Mr R. Wilding

Qualifications
  Degree
  Other	

Occupational experience	Sewing machine mechanic; sewing machine representative; technical adviser; sales manager; self-employed in retail/mail order business
Previous experience of product	Model craft business had provided relevant knowledge to start up EER Ltd as he was involved in purchase of batteries for use in conjunction with models sold from his shop
Product	Assembly of specialist battery packs Own brand packaging of rechargeable batteries
Business management experience	Acquired from previous employment and from operating own business

systems and for lighting. John Fawkes, through his involvement with an existing company, realized the potential and need for development of that company's product. He became

Table 2.5   Marlec Engineering Limited

Proprietor	Mr J.F. Fawkes

Qualifications
  Degree
  Other	

Occupational experience	Apprentice electrical engineer; development manager; company director
Previous experience of product	Gained through involvement with an existing company; Marlec is developing a product of that company
Product	Wind generators for electrical fencing systems
Business management experience	Gained during an 18-year period as director of Makron Engineering Co. Ltd

involved in its development and this led ultimately to the creation of Marlec Engineering, which is now extending the development of this product.

The occupational–product link is more indirect in this case. Here we have an entrepreneur made aware of the potential of a product, becoming involved in the company producing it and the experience gained from this leading to the creation of his own new company. Marlec Engineering is discussed in more detail on chapter 3.

Inhalation Therapy Products Limited (table 2.6) design and manufacture hospital consumables. The experience gained by the proprietor, Jeffrey Cresswell, enabling him to produce his company's product range, has clearly been obtained from his previous employment. He has an extensive employment background in the hospital supplies industry. This entrepreneur, by his involvement in the industry identified a range of products in demand by hospitals, and this combined with his own experience and skills enabled him to produce and supply these from his own business.

Pro Stock Glass Limited (table 2.7), proprietors Robert Dimmick and Allan Pentecost, manufacture, supply and

Table 2.6   Inhalation Therapy Products Limited

Proprietor	Mr J.R. Cresswell
Qualifications	
Degree	
Other	HNC Electrical Engineering
Occupational experience	Managing director; general manager; marketing manager; sales manager; technical services manager; special projects manager; service manager; design/development engineer
Previous experience of product	Gained from previous employment
Product	Design and manufacture of hospital consumables
Business management experience	Training in the area of marketing and financial control, practical experience through previous employment

Table 2.7   Pro Stock Glass Limited

Proprietor	Mr R.A. Dimmick (RAD) Mr A.G. Pentecost (AGP)
Qualifications Degree Other	 RAD – City and Guilds Industrial Refinishing AGP – New Zealand Trade Board for Tool Makers Engineering Design
Occupational experience	RAD – Apprentice coach painter; area salesman motor factors; technical rep. body panel and paint suppliers; speciality salesman; commercial diver with offshore oil company AGP – Engineering apprentice toolmaker; racing car mechanic; glass fibre racing car bodies and mould design
Previous experience of product	Predominantly based on previous employment of AGP
Product	Design, manufacture and supply of glass fibre bolt-on panels for racing/stock car market and for DIY motor enthusiast, including advising on handling and suspension technical problems
Business management experience	Gained only from running Pro Stock

design glass fibre bolt-on body panels for the racing/stock car market and generally for DIY motor car enthusiasts. They also advise on various handling and suspension technical problems. Pro Stock's range of products depend very much upon the previous occupational experience of Allan Pentecost. Robert Dimmick's present responsibilities lie predominantly on the sales and management side. A clear link again exists here between a proprietor's previous occupational experience and the products being produced.

Light Fantastic (table 2.8), produce and market holograms. The entrepreneur, Peter Woodd, probably has the most extensive educational background of all. He has received formal business training and has an HNC in mechanical

Table 2.8　Light Fantastic

Proprietor	Mr P.H.L. Woodd
Qualifications	
Degree	
Other	HNC Mechanical Engineering; HNC Business Studies; Postgraduate diploma in management studies
Occupational experience	Aerospace industry – business management on international contracts to supply defence systems to NATO countries; general manager of holography company
Previous experience of product	Gained from previous employment
Product	Production and marketing of holograms
Business management experience	Formal qualifications in business field and practical management experience in previous employment

engineering. The experience of the product itself has been gained from Peter Woodd's previous employment and business experience. Until February 1981, before creating Light Fantastic, he had total responsibility for developing the

Table 2.9　Victoria East Limited

Proprietor	Ms V. East
Qualifications	
Degree	
Other	
Occupational experience	Personal assistant to directors of several large companies
Previous experience of product	None in this area; self-taught designer with natural design talent
Product	Design and manufacture of high quality Christmas stockings; now extended to gift bags, toy bags and shoe bags
Business management experience	Limited training gained on secretarial course. Some knowledge gained from observation and practical experience in previous employment

commercial potential of holography with the largest company in this area, being both a shareholder and a director at the same time.

Victoria East (table 2.9) design and manufacture high quality Christmas stockings. The proprietor, Victoria East, has expanded recently into the design and manufacture of gift bags, toy bags and shoe bags.

This particular small business is an interesting case. Ms East was for some time a personal assistant to directors of several large companies, and while she has no formal design training and no previous employment history in this area, she is a self-taught designer who has shown a natural design flair. In this particular case the business is based upon the natural abilities of its proprietor and the occupational–product link does not seem to exist. Any practical managerial or business expertise she has acquired has been obtained vicariously through observation during previous employment.

Polstar Limited (table 2.10), proprietors Richard Lodge and James Snow, manufacture glass reinforced polyester products. This small business came into existence as a result of rationalization by a larger company. The two proprietors had been, prior to the creation of Polstar as such, the two

Table 2.10   Polstar Limited

Proprietor	Mr R. Lodge (RL)
	Mr J. Snow (JS)
Qualifications	
Degree	
Other	RL – ONC Engineering
Occupational experience	RL – Engineering apprenticeship; managing director
	JS – Trained as cabinet maker; works manager; manufacturing director
Previous experience of product	Both were directors of the firm they now own
Product	Glass reinforced polyester products
Business management experience	From previous employment and as directors of firm they now own

directors of this division of the larger company. Upon rationalization, the two directors decided to buy out this division to create Polstar. Once again a very clear occupational–product link exists, with the firm's two proprietors having extensive experience of the product and its market, and together putting this to good use for their own business.

Leather Fashions Limited (table 2.11), proprietors Delia Finn and James Finn, manufacture high fashion leatherware, mainly for women. These are sold through retail outlets and direct by mail order. Delia Finn has a degree in fashion textile design from a polytechnic and this represents the basis of the business. In addition, she has employment experience in this area. James Finn's training in graphics made the production of a mail order catalogue possible, and led to the mail order side of the business. Before Leather Fashions came into operation both proprietors had acquired experience of the product from operating a part-time business selling leatherware and selling these goods from market stalls and from operating a mail order business. The occupational–product link in this case is obviously a very extensive one.

Table 2.11 Leather Fashions Limited

Proprietor	Ms D. Finn (DF) Mr J. Finn (JF)

Qualifications
  Degree
  Other
	DF – Fashion Textile Design

Occupational
  experience
	DF – Fashion textile design
	JF – Engineering, training in
	    typography and graphic sales design

Previous experience
  of product
	Extensive, including training of DF
	  and her employment experience;
	  both operated part-time mail order
	  business

Product	High fashion leatherware, mainly for women

Business
  management
  experience
	Limited formal training; experience
	  acquired on learning-by-doing basis

Learning from Experience

Experience is the best teacher, says the proverb, but what exactly is it that our entrepreneurs have learned. What is the substance of the occupational link?

It is worth posing the question because there are several, sometimes overlapping answers. Or to put it a little differently, there is a mix of answers and the individual entrepreneurs vary in which part of that mix applies in particular cases.

First, there is clearly product knowledge. Several of our entrepreneurs have acquired this from their earlier experience. They know, that is, what the product is, how it is made or could be made, about the materials used and about the sort of improvements in methods, quality or end-product that customers would like. The proprietors of Inhalation Therapy Products, Polstar and Pro Stock are obvious examples. Then, taking this line of thought a little further, there is the related, experience-based ability to develop very much improved or even completely new products – for instance, Marlec Engineering, Optical Systems and Sycon Products.

Second, several of our entrepreneurs had already learned to sell, whether as retailers or manufacturers' representatives. The salesmen among the group include David Tillyard at Ensign Computers, Bryan Roberts at Sycon Products, Roger Wilding at Euro-Energy Resources, Jeffrey Cresswell at Inhalation Therapy Products and Robert Dimmick at Pro Stock.

Third, several of our sample have owned previous businesses – Bryan Roberts of Sycon Products, Roger Wilding of Euro Energy Resources and John Fawkes of Marlec Engineering are all cases in point. This guarantees that they will know about a range of practical things, such as the setting up of companies, the documentation, preparing accounts, administering PAYE, paying VAT and the formalities of employing people, as well as operating as credit arrangements, dealing with suppliers and handling customers.

Lastly there is a more general quality which several of the entrepreneurs have which we can perhaps formulate as 'knowing the trade'. Jeffrey Cresswell of Inhalation Therapy Products is a good example. He does not just know what the product is and how to sell it, he knows the trade too: that is, he knows who the customers are and what needs they have; he can identify rivals and knows the comparative price structures. David Tillyard at Ensign Computers is another example. He knows what computer programs can do, how to get hold of computers, how and what to sub-contract to software houses, what customers need and how to bring these all together.

The point at issue is that the occupational link is not only about product knowledge; it is about a variety of things, not all of which we will have succeeded in encapsulating here.

Signposts to Entrepreneurialism

It is interesting and important to emphasize this fact of practical occupational rather than formal educational experience. The successful operation and creation of a small business, and particularly so in our cases, seems to depend largely upon the skills acquired in regard to production methods, business contacts and retailing outlets, as well as more general skills – practical managerial skills, selling/ marketing skills and communication skills. These skills need not depend upon the intellect of the entrepreneur, but rather upon his or her personal characteristics and occupational background.

So what conclusions can we draw? If one wishes to raise the level of small business creation, then it would appear from our study that bigger doses of formal education, on its own, will not help. At least the connection between formal education and business success is not strong; it seems to hold only for some manufacturing industry rather than for business enterprise in general, and it is probably only critical for a narrow range of high technology industries. At the same time the advantages conferred by education are obvious. So where does this lead us?

The answer is that it points to the desirability of combining education with occupational experience. It is an argument in favour of work experience schemes at school and later, for 'thin' and 'thick' sandwich courses, for later entry to university or polytechnic, for employment between degrees and so on. In our view, it is particularly critical for more people who go to university to get some work experience; without it, whole sections of the most talented part of the age group are being pre-destined to salaried employee status in large organizations. Only the extremes of frustration or inspiration will deflect them from this course.

Notes

1 D.J. Storey, *Entrepreneurship and the New Firm* (Croom Helm, London, 1982).
2 E.B. Roberts and H.A. Wainer, 'New enterprises on Route 128' *Science Journal*, December (1968), pp. 78–83.
3 B. Nicholson and I. Brinkley, 'Entrepreneurial characteristics and the development of new manufacturing enterprises', paper given at a Centre for Environmental Studies conference on 'New firms in logical and regional economies', October 1979.
4 J. Boswell, *The Rise and Decline of Small Firms* (Allen & Unwin, London, 1972).
5 G. Gudgin, I. Brunskill and S. Fothergill, 'New manufacturing firms in regional employment growth', (Centre for Environmental Studies, 1979), Research Series no. 39.
6 Storey, *Entrepreneurship*.

3 The Engineering Dimension

This chapter will focus on Marlec Engineering and its founder, and will develop a number of ideas about engineering and its relationship to business success.

The backdrop to this story is the much-published malaise of manufacturing in Britain and the neglect of the engineering dimension. Against this backdrop, and with the focus on Marlec, we will develop the following ideas:

- it is possible for a technically innovative person to 'beat the system' even though the cards are stacked against the engineer; but it will not happen routinely, or in large numbers;
- for many businesses the concept of 'Technik' comes first; it is about making products not making money – if the first is done well the second may ensue;
- the engineering understanding is holistic; it cannot for the most part be bought-in. What the designer–developer–maker does implies a knowledge and scanning of many alternatives.

The Businessman–Engineer

It is clear that a strong engineering sector will remain important for the health of the British economy in the immediate future. Whatever the long term contribution may be, manufactured goods still account for nearly 60 per cent of the non-oil trade. Likewise, competition for manufactures will increase in home and export markets. Even in the recent past we have seen a growth in imports right across the board from basic heavy engineering goods to high technology products. If there is to be any reversal of this trend, then all the engineering sectors will have to play their part, including the small business sector.

There is what we might call a non-symmetrical relationship between engineering and business skills. Most small scale engineering enterprises provide the entrepreneur with the opportunity and the motivation to both develop technical skills and to learn or rehearse managerial skills. Sometimes the standard of these management skills has been criticized, yet it should be relatively easy to sensitize the engineer to the nature of the finance and marketing functions, using modern methods.

On the other hand, it is unlikely that a general business background could provide a suitable basis for the development of technical abilities for the successful conception, development, production and marketing of innovative engineering products on a continuing basis.

The Engineering Problem

The British engineering industry has declined in competitiveness although Britain still enjoys a reputation for innovative and successful research. What is more, there is growing evidence of coordinated national programmes for moving technologically up-market in a systematic way.[1]

It has also been argued[2,3] that our highly developed educational base could be focused rather more directly upon the needs of industry. These sorts of developments may indeed lead to an improvement in industrial performance.

Yet the decline in the performance of companies that are the very bedrock of engineering has been far too rapid and pronounced for anyone to be confident that such prescriptions will automatically regenerate our manufacturing sector, even on the basis of high technology products. It is not merely a question of reversing negative attitudes to industry in general and engineering in particular; neither has typically enjoyed the greatest social cachet in Britain. It is not enough to encourage our brightest and ablest to seek to develop their careers in a brave new high technology future. The fact is that the great bulk of the population, a high proportion of those involved in education, and an overwhelming proportion of those leading public opinion through the media, are technologically illiterate. With few exceptions engineering excellence goes unrecognized.

Engineering excellence, however, is actually an omnibus notion. It includes excellence in the conception of new product ideas, in the design of the product, in production engineering, in engineering quality and reliability into the product for an acceptable cost, and even in timing the introduction of marketable products. It would be wrong not to recognize the holistic nature of this process, and yet this is just what our cultural heritage tends to encourage.

There is no British equivalent to, for example, the pervasive influence of the idea of *Technik* in West Germany. The word *Technik* is used in that country to dignify the totality of engineering knowledge and skills to the point where organizational hierarchy is transcended, the idea of management as a separate entity is much less pronounced and the technical functions in industry enjoy a cultural umbrella.[4] Instead, every conceivable cleavage tends to be accentuated in Britain, not only social divisions, but divisions between functions and departments in the larger manufacturing companies. This is desperately ironic in an engineering context where the overall nature of the task dooms to mediocrity any piecemeal involvement.

There are not many people whose abilities, technical and social, result in upward mobility from, say, fitter to manager, while at the same time retaining an overall view of the engineering process. How much more likely that the gifted individual at all levels becomes frustrated within a culture where social, technical and managerial demarcations constrain rather than facilitate activity. Anyone who has experienced real frustration in being denied the opportunity of making a full contribution in an engineering company will know that, when repeated across the organization, this alone is likely to be the most damaging single factor to the development of excellence in bringing the company products to market.

Most frustrated employees will react against this climate of splintered functionalism, at any rate at first. But the eventual outcome may well be a withdrawal of a sense of responsibility. It may then be difficult to establish responsibility for missed deadlines, for poor product quality, for un-met delivery promises, for vacuous marketing efforts, for incompetent strategic development. Of course the cycle of irresponsibility will be broken every so often by individuals with particular character: Jaguar cars provide a good example of a company pulled back from the brink of extinction by enlightened management. But we are concerned here with the small proportion of frustrated employees who leave in order to develop an independent business.

It is probably at least as difficult to run a small engineering company as to run a small business in any other sector. The decline of engineering, after all, continues apace. The professionals and institutions with whom the proprietor must interact are, with few exceptions, at a distance culturally. The bank manager, for example, is much more likely to comprehend a plan for a hairdressing salon, and thus be capable of assessing the risk of lending. Or again, the accountant rarely has any technological training or insight.

Furthermore, the engineering employee is unlikely to have been encouraged to develop his general management skills before 'going solo'. Engineers are not expected to be articulate or to make much use of whatever personal talents they do possess. Yet if we know anything about education, it must be that expectation of a pupil's ability is a powerful determinant of actual achievement; that a self-fulfilling prophecy operates. Engineers may have had comparatively little opportunity to develop communication skills, yet these skills, or more precisely the lack of such skills, will quickly colour the attitude of the bank manager and the accountant.

Again, the engineering employee may have had very little experience of financial matters. Few engineers are expected to be competent at routine accountancy procedures, at say break-even analysis, or to be knowledgeable about the details

of venture capital schemes. Yet most small business proprietors will be involved in capital expenditure, the control of
working capital and the management of all-important cash
flows.

These tasks would seem to set the minimum skill levels
even for those who intend to set up as 'specialists'[5] – that
group of manufacturers or processors who supply a specific
market niche, usually as a result of some narrow in-house
technical expertise. If the business is stable, then so much the
easier to formulate a realistic business plan.

The problems facing would be 'jobbers' multiply rapidly.
This is because jobbers work on products made to the various
specifications of a number of customers. Whereas this may
spread the risk of dependence upon a single customer, the
bank manager is not going to be impressed by a failure to
conduct an analysis of future market opportunities. Yet
where has our putative engineering entrepreneur rehearsed
the necessary skills? It is unlikely that his former employer
would have delegated such responsibility to an engineer in
competition perhaps with an established market research
section.   What we here call the 'marketeer' faces the most
daunting challenge. He aims to produce, for sale to all-
comers, products to his own designs. This will involve
product conception and development in the first place, and
of course the capacity to produce the product to a marketable
standard of quality, at an acceptable price, to appropriate
time scales and in suitable volume. These engineering skills
must be matched by business skills. The marketeer will have
to find venture capital, attain financial control and organize a
sales and marketing effort.

The marketeer is thus involved on a broad engineering and
managerial front which must leave him comparatively
vulnerable. He will be fortunate if his bank manager is able to
appreciate the intellectual and practical achievements of
careful product development, and he will certainly not be at
all impressed if there is a technical hitch. The bank manager
will be out of his depth if he has to form an assessment of the
risk of further lending.

Given these gloomy considerations, one may well wonder
how the small engineering company ever manages to

prosper, let alone get off the ground. So to show that it is possible we will look at Marlec Engineering in more detail.

One Company's Experience

John Fawkes, the propietor, left school at the age of 14 and began his electrical engineering apprenticeship at a firm in Lincolnshire. This company made electrical generators, which were used for both primary and standby energy generation in ships and factories. Due to the higher demand and greater profit on the larger machines, the production of the smaller machines was discontinued. John Fawkes, by this time a foreman, tried to resist this change but without success. He and one of his colleagues believed there was a healthy market for the smaller generators, and so they decided, more out of frustration than anything else, to set up their own business.

In 1962 both men raised £250 each as venture capital[6] and established an engineering company. The beginnings were very humble; the business premises consisted of a garden shed and a garage. None the less, the demand for the generators grew rapidly. In the early 1960s companies could get financial assistance from a government-sponsored body called Rural Industries (the forerunner to the present Council for Small Industries in Rural Areas, or CoSIRA), and money was borrowed at a very attractive rate of interest to purchase a factory. Loans were also arranged for equipment and working capital.

With the continuing increase in demand for their products the company was in danger of 'overtrading' (see chapter 7); that is, their production and marketing activities were outstripping the capabilities of the firm's working capital. By 1965 the firm desperately needed more funds and so an approach was made to the Industrial and Commercial Finance Corporation (ICFC) which, for a 20 per cent share option, loaned £50,000.[7] Factories were opened in Inverness and Glasgow in 1966, and a factory in Sydney, Australia followed in 1967. The great demand for the products abroad was satisfied by a network of worldwide agents, whose performance contributed to the company's exporting achievements. This performance abroad was recognized in 1969, when the company received the Queen's Award to Industry.[8]

In 1973 a Nottinghamshire-based company which manufactured hydraulic mining equipment made a successful takeover bid.

As part of the takeover deal the two partners were required to stay on in a consultative capacity for three years after the takeover. In fact, Fawkes continued to be employed by them for the three years stipulated plus an additional four years. It was during this period that Fawkes experienced once more the need to be in the 'thick of things' where he was actually producing something, rather than attending meetings. Therefore, he was very pleased to be approached in 1980 by the proprietor of a company which made and supplied the components used in electric fencing systems. At that time many remote electric fencing systems were powered by battery. This had two disadvantages: first, the size of battery was limited by the problem of physically lifting it into place and so the current actually flowing through the fence was fairly low; and second, the batteries had a very short life before recharging was necessary.

It became clear that a wind-powered generator would overcome these two distinct disadvantages of existing electric fencing systems. The wind powered generator could recharge higher capacity batteries, thus increasing the current flowing through the fence, provided there was some wind. Fawkes set up a new company to manufacture wind generators – once more the premises were a garden shed. Development proceeded systematically and the company moved into a unit on an industrial estate in 1981.

The original size of the generator was determined by the amount of electrical power required to charge a 12 volt battery for electric fencing applications – some 50 watts – and this product remains the basis of the company's range. Since Fawkes had trained as an electrical engineer he had a thorough grasp of the technology involved and some idea of the problems that lay ahead. Existing wind-powered generators of a similar size from the United States and Canada, for example, required wind speeds of up to 10 mph before electricity was generated. Fawkes designed a generator in which this 'cogging' or 'striction' effect, the resistance that has to be overcome for the generator to start working, was drastically reduced, allowing electricity generation to be started up at very low wind speeds of around 4 mph. This deserves credit on two counts: an important design objective was established and then translated into actuality.

The development of the machine was performed very much on a trial and error basis, and once the optimum design was found the home-made machine tools used in the development were replaced with professionally made tools whose specifications were drawn up by a part-time draughts-man.

Even a quite small product such as the Marlec generator embodies many different parts fashioned from different materials. Choosing both implies a wide ranging knowledge of the pros and cons of various alternatives.

This product in fact incorporates bought-in aluminium castings, mild steel pressings, nylon blades, stainless steel fastenings, ball bearings, ceramic magnets, rectifiers and several other proprietary items. Some post processing is required on bought-in items; the nylon fan blades, for example, are subjected to a stress-relieving process on site, but the aluminium castings are sent out to a specialist local engineer for minor machining operations. The rotor hub, which embodies the generator, is built up in-house; the coils are wound, the magnets energized and the hub itself is formed from thermo-setting dough moulding compound. Other electrical components such as the rectifier, brushes and slip rings are assembled to a choke, which is wound on site. Great care is taken with what are called rotational balance and electrical integrity, and rigorous standards are set for testing intermediate steps in the assembly process, not leaving inspection for the end. The unit is packed for dispatch into two cardboard boxes, leaving the customer to assemble the nylon blades onto the hub with set screws, and to bolt on the tail fan.

To accomplish all this the company employs four young people, with an average age of 18 years, and Fawkes himself spends around a quarter of his time on front line supervision of the production process. The tools and jigs are improved from time to time to enable increasing output to be obtained with the same number of employees. All the employees do a range of different jobs in the production process, although one, a young girl, has additional secretarial functions and also deals with inputs to the micro computer. This is used, among other things, for production control and stock control of raw materials and bought-in items.

Great care is taken with quality control and during the three years prior to the study the number of wind chargers returned with manufacturing defects was nil! Each unit is fully guaranteed for one year, and service experience has been better than expected. This is also a reflection of the high standard of mechanical design, the careful specification of a range of metals and plastics, and considerable expertise in the detailed design of the generator.

John Fawkes has enjoyed modifying the product in response to requests by customers for help in specific circumstances. The so-called 'Furlmatic' variant has an automatic furling device which turns the generator out of the wind as it approaches its limits. This is particularly important because previous wind generators have always tended to self-destruct or burn out in high winds. The 'Marine' version has a number of special features which reduce the transmission of vibration to the hull and superstructure of small boats. The design has also withstood exposure to the particularly harsh and corrosive conditions experienced on ocean crossings.

The company buys in and supplies the very latest design of domestic fluorescent lighting equipment, which is several times more efficient than the traditional filament lights. These lights are installed in a specially manufactured casing which includes an invertor, made on site, allowing direct connection to a 12 volt battery. This allows the wind charger to be packaged and sold as a lighting system, either as a standby system in the event of power failure, or as a lighting system for remote communities.

The company spends only 2.5 per cent of sales turnover on direct advertising. Local press and specialist caravanning periodicals advertising bring in small orders, but the bulk of sales come through agents, mostly inherited from Fawkes' previous company which supplied alternators. There are 32 agents, of whom 29 are overseas. This is both a cause and reflection of the fact that over 86 per cent of output is exported.

There is also a wide range of applications for the wind charger:

- power to start up standby generators at an oil refinery;
- power for navigational buoys and warning lights at sea;
- power for remote telecommunications switching centres and television repeater stations;
- power for navigational and communication equipment on small boats;
- power to provide electricity in remote homesteads.

John Fawkes is a self-confessed poor salesman. Early and somewhat reluctant forays into trade shows generated considerable interest but not a single order. By contrast, many telephone orders are received each month from people throughout the world requesting information, but also placing orders based purely on other customers' recommendations. The proprietor plans to employ a publicity agent, who in his words, would really know how to sell the company 'and what it stands for'.

John Fawkes also realizes that it is high time to form a marketing plan. Using overseas agents, for example, has not been without problems. The company was owed some £20,000 by its South African agent who, in turn, had experienced a £10,000 bad debt (a customer shot by guerillas). There were risks in continuing to supply this agent and hoping that he would eventually supply the amount due, but the alternative would have been a real setback in the form of a loss of a significant market. John Fawkes intends to concentrate on formulating plans for rigorous marketing to the well-defined market sectors.

According to the Bolton Committee:[9]

Most small manufacturers are product-orientated and they are inclined to concentrate on the design and production of goods at the expense of proper attention to the crucial marketing function. In consequence, opportunities for expansion and for specialization or diversification may be missed and firms may find themselves trapped in a declining market, or at best tossed around by the ebb and flow of a fluctuating order book . . .

The potential markets in this instance appear to be large, and penetration has been moderately successful. The company is becoming conspicuously successful on an international basis, and this will no doubt attract others to develop similar machines. Not only should the market be large enough for several companies, but the individual sectors are taking on specific characters.

John Fawkes has every intention, and the necessary skills, to ensure that his products remain to the fore in any comparison of specifications for the foreseeable future. There seems little threat from the emerging technologies, such as photo voltaic cells. The costs, watt for watt, are significantly different and, if anything, the technologies are complementary rather than competitive as they utilize different sources of renewable energy. However, John Fawkes does recognize the need to move the company to a clearer definition of its objectives, and in particular its marketing plans. The product orientation remains healthily strong, and a new product has been projected for a completely new market.

Marlec purchased a small business micro computer early in 1983, and the standard accounting software which was supplied included a sales ledger, a purchase ledger, a nominal ledger, and stock control programs. John Fawkes was never over-keen on anything to do with accounting or management information systems in his previous company, and the microcomputer appealed to him primarily because it seemed to offer in-house control for very little effort. The programs were not without their teething problems, however, and it took a few days of outside assistance commissioned from the Loughborough University Department of Management before their full promise could be realized. John Fawkes now enjoys being in control of work in progress, stock, debtors and cash.

The system has greatly improved the cash flow from debtors and saves time on the completion of VAT returns. Other useful features of the sales ledger program include, albeit rudimentary, sales analysis, and interface with the nominal ledger which allows the production of the final accounts. The purchase ledger also interfaces into the nominal ledger to produce all the expense items that go into the profit and loss account, and the balance sheet. John Fawkes now produces both of these the day after the end of the month, which brings him a great deal of direct control. The stock control program makes it very easy to obtain raw material costings, and as a result the variable costs. John Fawkes has found it easy to do break-even and contribution analysis. He is presently receiving assistance under the auspices of the Small Firms Advisory Service in setting up a full costing system using a labour overhead rate. It is worth emphasizing the relative ease with which these systems have been applied *after* commercial success though engineering excellence has been achieved.

In short, John Fawkes, a one-time foreman, has established a new company in the renewable energy sector. The product is innovative and internationally successful because it is soundly developed, very well made and highly praised by existing users. The company is successful partly because John Fawkes is orientated to producing a machine with a better specification than its competition, but also because he has shown himself capable of coming to grips with product costing, management accounting, cash management and financial accounting. This is an unusual conjunction of skills and there is little reason to doubt John Fawkes's growing expertise in setting his company upon a secure trading footing.

Small but Significant

It has become customary, with honourable exceptions, to accept a somewhat defeatist attitude to the nation's failure to compete in the market for manufactures at home and abroad. Many see a future for a more highly developed service-based industry, exporting financial services such as insurance or investment advice. At home there would be growing markets for leisure services, and the provision of care and attention for our ageing population. In this scenario the future for manufactures is thought by some to be almost exclusively in high value, high technology products, from fibreoptics-based communication systems through to sophisticated armaments.

Our conviction, however, is that a thriving small manufacturing sector is one important ingredient for a successful national economy: there is a need to provide jobs quickly and cheaply; the volume of imports is a major economic problem; small business has a good record of innovation. A proportion of the small manufacturing concerns will grow in size and significance. Frustrated employees get the opportunity to escape a functional specialism and to develop a general business capability.

The 'high technology' label may have had the unfortunate effect of drawing attention away from the less glamorous bedrock of innovative engineering generally, which Marlec represents. The innovation may be in the development of a new product idea, in utilizing new materials, in adopting 'low technology' process techniques such as pneumatics or in the incorporation of 'high technology' micro electronics, for example. The fundamental point about a technology is its over all nature and not just whether a particular product embodies a micro electronic control system, for example. Furthermore, there can be little expectation of bringing new technology to market without the skills that are necessary in the manufacture and marketing of, for example, products with a high content of traditional mechanical engineering skills.

The Moral of the Story

The Marlec story is a good story, and a success story; but it is more than this. It shows that the barriers can be broken, and engineering excellence achieved. At the same time, more than a word of warning is needed.

This entrepreneur is not picked at random from the ranks of the talented and frustrated. He has already founded one company and succeeded to the point of being bought out, and that success came in the much easier era of the 1960s. In other words, this small businessman had the advantage of pre-existing capital, contacts and confidence.

Marlec is also a study in the virtues of holism – one person combining ingenuity and control, patience and inventiveness, a knowledge of methods and alternative materials and an understanding of the importance of quality and how to get it. If the divisiveness of English society is often paralleled in larger companies by a division of the technical whole, then Marlec shows, albeit in miniature, what the alternative looks like.

Finally, we have suggested that Marlec's founder is favoured by his past. So he is, and the supply of people with that degree of talent will always be limited. Neither consideration need lead to fatalism, however. If it can be done once, it can be done, and national efforts should concentrate on making it happen more often.

Notes

1 A Programme for Advanced Information Technology, A Report of the Alvey Committee (HMSO, London, 1982).
2 Finniston Report, Engineering Our Future, (HMSO, London, 1980), cmnd 7794.
3 GEEP, Goals of Engineering Education, Final Report, (Leicester Polytechnic, 1983).
4 S.P. Hutton and P.A. Lawrence, *German Engineers: The Anatomy of a Profession*, (Oxford University Press, 1981).

5 H. Lydell, 'Aspects of competition in manufacturing industry', *Bulletin of the Oxford Institute of Statistics*, November 1978; cited by A. Adams, in 'Barriers to product innovation in small firms: policy implications', *European Small Business Journal*, 1 (1982), no. 1.

6 This is approximately equivalent to £1,500 at 1984 prices.

7 Approximately £300,000 at 1984 prices.

8 This was a scheme launched in 1965 to recognize outstanding achievement by British industrial firms in either export or technological development.

9 Bolton Report, 'Report of the Committe of Inquiry on Small Firms', (HMSO, London, 1971), cmnd 4811.

4 A Buy-out: Context and Consequences

A success story of a different kind is the subject of this chapter. It recounts the circumstances that led to a management buy-out and what happened to the new company after the event.

A management buy-out is where a manager or managers working for a company buy part of the company from its owners and proceed to run it as their own rather than as employed managers. The incidence of buy-outs increased with the recession that began in 1980, the typical buy-out being precipitated by companies in difficulties deciding to close some factory, plant, or operation to get ready money or to avert some loss, and managers in the affected part of the business responding by trying to raise enough money to buy it and keep the entity going.

There are several themes to be explored here. First it is interesting to show what led to this particular buy-out – not a simple business failure by the existing company but rather a cumulation of vicissitudes. Secondly, the buy-out itself is worth exploring both in relation to its terms and conditions and to the factors that seem to have led to a successful negotiation. By no means all management buy-out initiatives lead to successfully acquired part-companies, nor are buy-out deals invariably a simple matter of the buyer meeting the seller's asking price. Thirdly the tacit assumption is that the cards are stacked against the buy-out initiators' making a success of the company they acquire: after all, if there are not real problems about running this operation, why does the present owner want to close or sell it, and why should the newly acquiring managers make a better job of it; after all they have not had entrepreneurial experience before? In this account we want to show how and why the new owners succeeded, and to redress the balance by underlining the advantages that accrue to the new owners after a management buy-out.

Background History

The company which is the subject of our story was founded by a single proprietor just after the Second World War in the south-west of England. In the early 1960s it opened a new works in the Newcastle upon Tyne area, and with this addition the company, as originally founded, lasted until 1968.

The work of this company was glass reinforced polyester products, with the product range divided into two – standard sheeting, in various shapes and sizes, and a more decorative range of products, used for ornamental work on shop fronts, banks and so on, and some work, coats of arms, insignia etc. involving an element of heraldry. Much of this latter activity was of a one-off variety demanding considerable skills in manufacture and a careful and somewhat subjective estimating procedure. The base raw materials of these two product categories were identical, but the manufacturing practices and skills, and the consequent demands on management, were quite different.

The company remained privately owned until 1968, at which time it was bought out by a publicly quoted company, Walton–Brock, involved in a different line of business and with its main works in the south-east. By this time James Snow, one of the subsequent proprietors of Polstar as it became, was working for the company. Snow, a local Newcastle man who had trained as a cabinet-maker, was works manager, and had been with the company for many years. Richard Lodge, the other subsequent proprietor, joined the company a number of years later after working for a manufacturer of heating and sanitary ware. Snow had no formal qualifications beyond his apprenticeship (cf. tables

2.1–2.11), while Lodge had served an engineering apprenticeship and gained an Ordinary National Diploma. He is also a natural linguist, with fluent Swedish and a working knowledge of German.

After 1968 the new owners put in their own managing director, the original proprietor having gone into retirement, and this MD stayed until 1972. James Snow did not especially like this MD and had doubts about some of the moves the company made during this 1968–72 period. The first was to move from modest to somewhat larger premises, from a floor space of 6,000 sq ft to one of 20,000 sq ft; the second was at the same time a move from owned premises to rented accommodation; and the third was doing both of these on the basis of a small order book.

In 1972 this MD left, the parent company advertised for a general manager and Richard Lodge applied for and got the post. For the first years, 1972- , the company just managed to break even, 1976 saw a small profit and by 1979-80 the company showed a good return on capital employed. It became the 'blue-eyed boy' of the parent company. By this time Richard Lodge was managing director and James Snow manufacturing director. Also, by the same period, the parent company, Walton–Brock, was having difficulties of its own. Although a public company, it was dominated by two families who did not really gel. The chairman made a tour of North America and embarked on what turned out to be a series of catastrophic investments. The inevitable crisis came at the end of the decade when one of the major shareholders, a financial institution, put in a nominee director. By early 1980 the former chairman had been removed and a new board of directors appointed.

Meanwhile the polyester company, still doing well under Lodge and Snow, started to feel the effect of these changes. It is the all too familiar story of near collapse, new direction at the centre, followed by an orgy of controls and information gathering. But implementing controls and assembling a management information system costs.

This is how it appeared to Richard Lodge, running his works in Newcastle: 'At this time, and I am not a good delegator anyway, I got lumbered with an accountant, then a cost accountant, then a secretary to the accountant and all to provide a management base for the 1980s.'

The effect was to push overheads to £1m a year, while turnover (value of sales) fell from £1.2 million to £0.9 million (the 1980 recession had started).

The next and critical development was that the new board decided to concentrate the sheeting manufacture at the Newcastle works, while at the same time withdrawing from the decorative work. They did not want Richard Lodge to head this operation. He was offered a sales directorship elsewhere in the empire (which he declined as it would have meant moving to the Midlands) while James Snow was simply offered redundancy. Neither director wanted what was offered them and both wanted to see the decorative work continue, believing (rightly) that it had a future. In consequence, they began negotiations with Walton–Brock for the purchase of the decorative side of the business. These negotiations were eventually successful and the new firm, Polstar, came into existence in the autumn of 1980.

We have told the story in full precisely because it is more complicated than anyone unconnected with the world of business might expect. What emerges is a fascinating cumulation of 'ifs' and 'buts'. *If* the business as originally founded had not developed into the two product arms of sheeting and decorative, with their different requirements and operating attractions; *if* Walton–Brock had not acquired the original company; *if* they had not got into difficulties themselves; *if* Richard Lodge had been more of an infor- mation and systems man; *if* the owners had made Snow and Lodge different offers; *if* they had seen the merit of building up the decorative side of the business rather than going for the standardization and big order throughput of the sheet- ing...

The Polstar Buy-out

The buy-out negotiations began in May 1980 and lasted two months. Throughout this period no other potential buyers except Lodge and Snow came forward. This was probably because the operation of a specialist form of manufacture required not only the technical know-how of production and, more importantly, of pricing, but also because the trade contacts with customers are vital to survival.

One of the typical problems of the attempted buy-out, raising the capital for the purchase price, was circumvented in this case. The usual scramble of the managers concerned to raise second mortgages on their houses and, in extremis, pull their children out of fee-paying schools for the greater good of British entrepreneurialism was bypassed. The seller offered the purchase money as an interest-free loan to be repaid over two years.

The sum involved, £58,000, was agreed as an appropriate payment covering plant, machinery, stock, work-in-progress and goodwill. This would, therefore, provide everything except the premises and the workforce to operate the facilities.

Although Lodge and Snow were not required to pay interest on the loan the agreement did include provision for a commission on sales to be paid to Walton–Brock by the new owners of Polstar. This was set at 10 per cent for the first year, 5 per cent for the second, and none thereafter.

A paradoxical situation began to emerge with the buy-out. Here were two companies operating in different products and markets: Walton–Brock in sheeting, Polstar in decorative products. At the same time, both were using the same raw materials and both had experience in the other's market. This again required some regulation, so it was agreed between the parties at the time of the buy-out that for the first three years the two sides would respect fully each other's interests in their respective operations and markets.

At first sight it might seem that Lodge and Snow got a good deal. Certainly by offering the purchase price as a loan, and an interest-free loan at that, the acquisition became possible for them, but consider the other side of the picture. In year one the new owners have to do well enough to pay back half of £58,000 and render a 10 per cent commission on sales, while at the same time respecting the interests of Walton–Brock and keeping out of the sheeting market. This represents a considerable challenge, and how the new owners responded will be described in a moment. First, let us have another look at the buy-out in terms of a different perspective.

The Model Buy-out

We suggested earlier that many buy-out initiatives, and for that matter purchase negotiations, come to nothing. Sue Birley has suggested a model for explaining the success or failure of such transactions in broad terms.[1] Calling on her experiences with management buy-outs, Sue Birley structures a three-dimensional conflict rubric; that is, she cites the three things that can lead to conflict in buy-out negotiations and therefore to their failure. By the same token a positive score on these three variables is likely to lead to success. The three variables are:

- seller motivation;
- buyer motivation;
- size of unit involved.

The Birley argument is that with a high level of seller benevolence, a positive attitude on the part of the would-be buyer and small size, the chance of conflict in the negotiations is much reduced, and this in turn should lead to a successful deal. A successful (post buy-out) firm does not necessarily follow from a successful deal, and we aim to deal separately with the question of Polstar's success shortly. Let us first consider Birley's three variables. It is important to underline the fact that the first two – seller and buyer motivation – can by no means be taken for granted. The parent company is often quite unwilling to sell, preferring the extinction of the unit to its continuation under other ownership, and to be fair there may be good business policy reasons for this. Again, the parent company may resent the implied criticism/arrogance of the would-be buyers, who are saying in effect that the unit has a good future under their inspired direction once the dead-hand of the down-beat owner has been removed.

Buyer motivation may also be less than wholehearted and resolute. Frequently management buy-out initiatives are born of fear and desperation. Imagine you are a middle-aged manager employed by a reputable company. One week you have status, income, a comfortable life style, the next week closure of your part of the firm is threatened and you have nothing to look forward to except a redundancy package. In circumstances ôf this kind the buy-out option is bound to be considered, but many prospective buyers 'back off' when they discover the asking price and what one would have to do to raise it. It is one thing to want something, another to want it badly enough to sell your car, risk losing your home and padlock the drinks cabinet! It is against this kind of backdrop that we should view the Walton–Brock and Polstar deal.

The seller motivation in this case is reasonably high. Sue Birley proposes that seller motivation should be graded as high, medium or low. On this basis the seller motivation of Walton–Brock is at least medium. The parent has decided to divest itself of the decorative range anyway, views it as a relatively unimportant part of its overall activities, and has no reason to be threatened by the perpetuation of the decorative part of the business. Bear in mind too that they are clearly not hostile to Richard Lodge as an individual either. He came in as general manager in the wake of a spendthrift MD, exercised good husbandry for several years and then started to get them a good return on capital employed. They think well enough of him to offer him a decent job at a respectable level in the wider company, even if he does not choose to accept this offer. Seller benevolence must also be raised a little by the fact that the decision to divest of what became Polstar was all started by failures in the parent company itself, not in the polyester branch.

If we turn next to buyer motivation, Sue Birley again proposes three levels, this time labelled negative, neutral and positive. Negative motivation is when the managers do not really believe in the firm, or indeed in themselves, and only contemplate the buy-out against the background of dire alternatives. Neutral motivation implies that the managers concerned would actually prefer to run the subsidiary themselves, given that the decision to sell has been taken. Positive motivation, on the other hand, stems from a situation where, following a good relationship with the parent company, the management of the subsidiary wishes to seize an opportunity to advance its technical expertise, its knowledge of the market and its responsibility for company policy. In this instance the motivation of Lodge and Snow must be rated positive. They genuinely and correctly believed at the time of the buy-out that they could use their knowledge and abilities to preserve and expand the decorative side of the business.

The third variable of size refers both to the size/complexity of the negotiation as well as the size of the business which is the subject of the negotiation. The latter is indeed small (see discussion below on number and choice of employees), but it is worth considering further the scale and complexity of the negotiations. Complexity here refers most obviously to the number of parties involved, besides the buyer and seller. Inevitably lawyers and accountants will be involved, but at the extreme there could also be the company's bank, investors, market research consultants, trade unions, merchant banks, a receiver, investment trusts, family interests, and so on. The more involved the negotiation, the longer it is likely to take, the more are the opportunities for conflict and the greater the chance that both may jeopardize the vitality of the bought-out business. In the case of the present deal we see the whole negotiation between Lodge and Snow on the one side and Walton–Brock on the other completed in less than two months, and parties to those negotiations are limited. This together with the modest size of the entity created, Polstar, means we must rank this deal favourably on the size continuum. In short, in Birley's terms, the conditions for this buy-out, while not perfect, were generally favourable.

Polstar at Large

So far we have presented a piece of business history, outlining the development of a company from birth to the buy-out. We have looked at the buy-out itself, both examining the interest of particular terms and conditions and looking at the reasons for the success of the negotiations in a wider perspective. Next we look at the development of this company under its new owners.

At the time of the buy-out the existing premises were not for sale since Walton–Brock planned the concentration of the sheeting manufacture on this site. So the newly formed Polstar had to seek a suitable site, which they found in the form of a small rented factory in a small town outside Newcastle upon Tyne. When the tenancy agreement expired two years later they moved to more spacious premises (over 11,000 sq ft) in another town on the Newcastle periphery.

At the time of the Polstar start-up, Lodge and Snow took nine employees from the workforce of 82 at the old Newcastle factory, though if one restricts consideration to those workers on the decorative side of the original business, it was really nine out of 40. Not long after the founding of Polstar, Walton–Brock appointed a new MD of their sheeting works who in the event declined to come to Newcastle; by the autumn of the buy-out year Walton–Brock had decided to abandon their plan to enlarge the sheeting manufacture at the Newcastle site and concentrate it instead at another works in the West Midlands. This meant more Walton–Brock employees becoming available on the local labour market to the benefit of Lodge and Snow. From the start-up with nine workers they soon built up to 15 or 16 and more ex-Walton–Brock workers applied to them as soon as the news of Polstar's moving to larger premises came out. There are already some interesting clues to Polstar's success here.

Perhaps what connects these is the disposition of the two directors, who share many opinions. Not all entrepreneurs are like these two, but Richard Lodge in particular certainly represents *a* type, and one that is generally successful. Weak on delegation and strong on control, not taking risks that do not have to be taken, watching the pennies and getting value for money – from employees, deals, suppliers, even machines – and above all not loading up the company with any costly extras it does not need. We see these qualities right from the start: modest premises, move to something bigger when the orders warrant it; nine workers and two foremen taken from the Walton–Brock plant (carefully chosen of course), building up the labour force as the growing business warrants; and above all no redundant managers or costly systems. Five years after the buy-out Polstar was still run by Lodge and Snow, who had never taken on more managers.

In the autumn of 1980, at the time of the start-up, cash was important. In chapter 1 we described one of Polstar's coups in illustrating the role of 'the lucky break' in small business start-ups. Richard Lodge exploited an earlier business contact in Scandinavia, became sub-contractor for the decorative work on a major project, and was promised £32,000 on delivery by the principal contractor. One can do a lot worse than start like this.

If this Scandinavian deal is a little out of the ordinary, it is noticeable that various people 'went easy' on Polstar in the early stages where payment was concerned. Polstar's insurance brokers, for instance, defrayed the costs over three instalments. Suppliers were also inclined to be accommodating with regard to payment terms. There is clearly a pattern here, in that Walton–Brock having withdrawn from sheeting manufacture in the Newcastle area, suppliers were bound to welcome anyone attempting to continue (part of) the business.

The newly founded Polstar has not lacked for orders and has pursued a rational policy to bring about this happy state of affairs. At the start they identified a national retail chain, we will call it Multishop, as a key to success, because of its 'specifying power', that is, its ability to direct shopfitting contractors to have the decorative glass reinforced polyester work done by Polstar. Lodge and Snow, of course, already had dealings with Multishop in their Walton–Brock days. The difference is that Multishop had been regarded as a bit of a nuisance in that period with Walton–Brock's prime interest in the sheeting side of the business, whereas Polstar now set out to court and please Multishop, with highly satisfactory results. This has a further spin-off, namely that Multishop's architects are highly mobile. They go to work for other organizations and they also go independent. In either case, if they dealt with Polstar from their Multishop base, their later dispersal around the economy is bound to be beneficial in terms of sales leads and orders.

The second plank in the sales strategy was the production at an early stage of a good catalogue. The work of Polstar is decorative and visual and Polstar have emphasized quality, so putting it on display in a catalogue makes good sense. It is also a chance to advertise the fact of doing work for Multishop, especially complicated one-off jobs, as this is bound to lead to Polstar's being taken up by others.

The third plank has been the pursuit of a variety of other retail chains, all of which were known from Walton–Brock days, though again the relationship with them had not been especially close because of Walton–Brock's emphasis on sheeting production. All these chains have the famous 'power of specification', though none of them looms quite so largely in Polstar's fortunes as Multishop.

To the policy as described two bonuses should be added. In the spring of 1983 a significant competitor company failed, leaving among others Multishop with some unfilled orders. Here was yet another opportunity for Polstar to demonstrate quality of service to a major customer.

The second bonus derives in part from the technology and in part from traditionalism. The technical fact is that for the more elaborate decorative jobs a mould has to be made, and the 'mould-holder' is most likely to get all the repeat order business. To this may be added the fact that many overseas countries like to deal with Britain, especially her former colonies. Polstar is in the happy position of holding moulds for all sorts of emblems and coats of arms for a variety of banks, institutions and public utilities in a range of countries. Polstar has good relations with the Crown Agents and gets work and inquiries from the former colonies referred to it. Moreover this is a game where, periodically, time is on your side. Consider the fact that many African states are coming up for the twentieth anniversary of their independence. How better to commemorate it than with a (Polstar-fashioned) coat of arms?

Some of our companies have had difficulty with machinery or equipment. Difficulties in knowing what to buy, when the level of business warranted capital investment, or in simply finding the money. Polstar has managed well in this respect. The original deal with Walton–Brock gave Lodge and Snow the equipment relevant to the decorative work, and since the buy-out they have put in a dust extractor, an improved compressed air system, and built an extension to the second and larger factory. All this they have been able to pay for out of retained earnings. Their policy on more routine equipment acquisition, however, is an interesting manifestation of the value-for-money orientation referred to earlier. They do not buy new equipment: not to save laying out larger sums, but because the newer equipment is not deemed sound enough. They retain a preference for post Second World War equipment, or occasionally earlier models. They say manufacturers knew what they were doing in those days!

The buying of raw materials is often problematic for small firms,[2] yet again Polstar has fared well. We referred earlier to suppliers being accommodating in the start-up period to the advantage of the nascent company. Since those early days the problem Polstar has faced is avoiding the pressure from supplies to enter into continuity (of supply) agreements. They have resisted this pressure and are still buying spot. For the resins there are two or three suppliers who, at least at certain times of year, will make reductions for customers buying 5 tons, or sending the cheque with the order. Polstar's freedom from continuity agreements also makes it possible for them to go to new entrants to the supplier market and to experiment with new resins themselves. Polstar has also joined forces with another glass reinforced polyester company in order to buy raw materials in bigger lots. Polstar as well makes a practice of ringing round suppliers at the end of the month to see what discount they can get for cash. In other words, Polstar is taking all the tricks in the supply game.

Finally, Polstar offers an interesting understanding of the nature of product quality and is probably gaining a competitive edge here. For much of the engineering industry, and for many consumer goods industries, quality is about the state of the manufactured item before it leaves the factory – does it look right, does it work, does it conform to agreed specifications? This basic notion of quality is not irrelevant to Polstar's decorative work. The firm's general policy is to keep the price and material content up; they do not stint on 'the recipes', sometimes putting in more reinforcement than is specified and applying extra layers of gel coat to ensure a good finish. But this is not the whole story in the case of Polstar's decorative products. Quality is also about durability and weathering and therefore in taking post-delivery problems seriously. Polstar does not formally limit the guarantee to one year, and is ready to go out and explore any problems a customer may be experiencing. To this end the firm is also conscientious about keeping records of batch numbers for all the outgoing work.

Enough has been said to show that Polstar is successful and to illuminate some of the interlocking reasons. To return to our opening theme, it is interesting to see how many of Polstar's current operating strengths derive from the earlier association with the polyester part of Walton–Brock and from the buy-out situation itself. From these origins the two entrepreneurs variously enjoyed the pick of a known workforce, favourably disposed suppliers, critical trade contacts, including the most important sales leads, as well as some reactive views on pitfalls to be avoided. This is a good deal.

Polstar's pursuit of quality and good after-sales service, however, should be attributed to nothing but the new owners' good sense. Indeed it is interesting to see that the most successful firms in our sample of small businesses practise a policy of being, in the phrase made famous by Peters and Waterman, 'close to the customer'.[3]

Notes

1 S. Birley, 'Success and failure in managements', *Long Range Planning*, 17 (1980), pp.32–40.
2 For a discussion of the problem with suggested remedies, see Peter Lawrence and Robert Lee, *Insight into Management* (OUP, Oxford, 1984), ch.5.
3 Thomas J. Peters and Robert H. Waterman jun., *In Search of Excellence* (Harper & Row, New York, 1982).

5 A Study in Deflection

Terry Corner founded Optical Systems Limited in June 1983 with the prime objective of developing and marketing a high technology coordinate measuring machine. The company also had two further products: ophthalmic test charts and profile projectors. The coordinate measuring machine was innovative and Terry Corner won an award in the MIDAS 1983 Small Business Competition to promote its development. Fifteen months after the prize-giving, however, the company had not managed to make any progress on developing the coordinate measuring device, and through a series of disasters had in fact lost the market for ophthalmic test charts. When the authors last visited the company late in 1984 the proprietor was machining a batch of fishing reels which he hoped to sell locally, simply to generate a bit of income. Development plans which had seemed so desirable little more than a year earlier, were, at least temporarily, abandoned.

This chapter is not only about what happened to Terry Corner's plans, but also about the pressures and forces that often beset the small businessman. It explores in terms of an individual story the general theme of one of the often-attempted transitions from inventor to businessman. The account of Optical Systems Ltd also illustrates many of the characterizing propositions about making a small business breakthrough put forward in chapter 1, including the idea that the stories of these small firms are often surprisingly complicated.

Background to the Start-up

Institutions involved in the MIDAS competition, and thus invited to provide financial backing for Optical Systems Ltd in June 1983, were presented with the following case.

Terry Corner's background experience had been very much in engineering practice. Having left school in Derby at the age of 15, he served a basic engineering apprenticeship and later worked for a number of local engineering firms as fitter, toolmaker, foreman and works engineer. He joined Derby Optical Company in 1977 as manager of their instruments division, where he had responsibility for design and production of profile projectors and ophthalmic test charts. This is an impressive progression of job responsibility in both design and administration for someone whose qualifications had been derived mainly from practical experience.

Corner had real talent as an inventor. His great strengths were adaptation, modification and application; he had the imagination to improve on the models of competitors and the engineering experience to develop prototypes and to carry them through to the production stage; he had experience of production supervision and could actually make the products himself if need be. This was a lot to offer but, in fact, Corner had further valuable qualifications as a potential businessman. He also had established in the market place good contacts developed over a number of years' direct experience, and besides his innovative product he had two further products with established market potential: profile projectors and ophthalmic test charts. We will describe both of these in more detail later.

The new product, the coordinate measuring device, adapted some of the features of the profile projectors and was claimed to have several features that were in advance of anything else on the market. This product was, in fact, very much in the high technology field and, given the inventor's lack of formal education and training in science and technology, this may have given cause for concern to some prospective financiers. Corner, however, was without doubt

vastly more knowledgeable than the average trained fitter
and turner. Through various occupations he had demonstrated an ability to learn quickly and at Derby Optical
Company had designed new machinery and layouts as well
as coping with highly complex scientific developments. His
indomitable energy is shown by the fact that during this
same period he purchased an old property,a disused chapel,
and single-handedly restored and converted it into a beautiful home for his family.

Here was a young and vigorous would-be entrepreneur
with seemingly boundless energy and a great deal of relevant
expertise in his field. Granted he was lacking experience in
sales and even more so in finance, but with his proved ability
as a quick learner, it seemed reasonable to assume that he
could overcome that disability, given the time which a
cushion of sufficient start-up capital would provide.

At the date of the MIDAS Competition award, that is, June
1983, Corner had already made several successful steps
towards his objective.

1 He had put together a working prototype of his
   advanced new product; with most of the expensive
   components being borrowed from business contacts.
2 He had obtained basic business advice from the Department of Industry Small Business Advice Scheme.
3 He had prepared a business plan showing an estimated
   need for start-up capital of £60,000.
4 He had managed to raise £15,000 from his own
   resources.
5 He had submitted an application for a bank loan through
   the Small Business Loan Guarantee Scheme.
6 He had applied for a capital grant under the Department
   of Industry Support for Innovation Scheme and had
   received a favourable reply. (In fact he qualified for a
   grant of 33 per cent of the required start-up funds.)

It can be seen, therefore, that he had already demonstrated
a considerable amount of ability to stand alone in the
business world he was about to enter. The proposition was

still one of very high risk and the competition adjudicators were aware of this. Their concern about Terry Corner's lack of formal scientific qualifications was outweighed by the fact that his technical application under the Support for Innovation Scheme had been favourably received – success there was an indication that he had been able to convince technical experts of the feasibility of the new product and of his ability to carry it through.

As a business proposition therefore, Terry Corner's case as of June 1983 seemed to be quite a reasonable one. He had developed an existing new high technology product that seemed to have good prospects, and his company also had two established products that seemed to have a reasonably secure market – a market portfolio of which many small companies launching into the high technology field would be envious.

The idea for setting up Optical Systems Ltd arose when Corner's desire for invention and development suffered some frustration while he still worked for his prevous employer. He had conceived the idea for his advanced coordinate measuring machine while still with the Derby Optical Company Ltd but his employers were unable or unwilling to fund its development. So determined was he to pursue this development, however, that he decided to try to get financial backing to develop it himself. During the time he was negotiating for funds, another event occurred which pushed him further along the entrepreneurial road. The management of Derby Optical Company decided to cease production in the instrument division which Corner managed, and he was made redundant. He immediately negotiated with his former employers to take over production of their two basic products by setting up his own production facility to develop, manufacture and sell these products as well as the new high technology coordinate measuring machine. Meanwhile, in June 1983 Corner won the MIDAS Small Business Competition award for the latter and through this he qualified for £4,000 prize money, rent-free accommodation from Leicestershire County Council and free consultancy in marketing and finance. Several important components of his project were coming together very satisfactorily and he seemed to be on his way. However, the course of the small business entrepreneur rarely runs smooth, and Corner soon began to experience some very rough going.

Operations Commence

Winning the MIDAS award qualified Optical Systems Ltd for a cash prize of £4,000, rent-free accommodation for one year and subsidized accommodation for a further two years, plus some free consultancy.

To qualify for the award, Optical Systems Ltd had to set up operations within Leicestershire and, naturally, Corner had agreed to make the move if he should be a winner. However, from the beginning he found this need to move a traumatic experience. For his family's sake he wished to continue to live in Derby but was also loath to site the business too far away because he realized he would need to work long and irregular hours and was concerned about the demand which constant travelling would make on his time and energy. He therefore stipulated that he wanted premises in north-west Leicestershire and indeed the county council, as providers of his assisted accommodation, tried sympathetically to meet his need. They seemed to find great difficulty in doing so, however, because of a lack of suitable property in that area. This was especially frustrating for Terry Corner as he was aware of several sites in Derby which he considered ideal for his purpose and which were available for his immediate use at reasonable rents.

After several properties had been offered for consideration and turned down by Corner as unsuitable he eventually accepted a place in Shepshed near Loughborough – out of frustration, he claims, rather than satisfaction. The premises were indeed far from ideal. The structure resembled a very large barn, much of it of corrugated iron construction; its area was easily three times larger than that needed by Optical Systems Ltd and the roof was about 30 feet high so that winter heating bills would be astronomical if working conditions were to be tolerable; the building needed substantial repair. These were not ideal conditions to launch a new business nor the most attractive place to impress prospective clients, but at least they provided a base in which to set up production and Corner lost no time in moving in and setting up a facility to assemble the two basic products he had acquired from his former employers – the profile projectors and the ophthalmic test charts.

Profile projectors are extensively used in engineering and are particularly suited for the magnification and examination of objects with irregular contours, such as die stampings, or regular contours, such as gears and screw threads. An obvious alternative magnification method is through the use of a microscope and for one-off inspections this is superior; but for various reasons, one important one being operator fatigue in microscope use, profile projectors are often more suitable for routine inspection of certain products. There is, therefore, an established market for the projectors and Corner was convinced that the number of contacts he had established in the market place, together with the goodwill which his previous employer had earned and which Corner believed he was inheriting, would provide a stable basis for new orders.

The ophthalmic test charts are electronically controlled eye test systems which have a remote control facility and provide a very broad range of test exercises. The main users are opticians in the private sector and in hospitals. A variety of options is available to suit the needs of different users and consequently the product ranges in price from about £300 to £500. For this product also there seemed to be an established market. Derby Optical Company was keen to continue marketing a wooden version of the test chart and Corner had agreement with a sales agent in London to market the metal versions of the product at a commission rate of 20 per cent. The most expensive component of the test chart was the electronic control device and Corner had established a good relationship with a local supplier who had been in business for some years and seemed most reliable. The relationship was sufficiently trustful to warrant some discussion about the possibility of a joint venture between the supplier and Optical Systems Ltd by which the supplier would invest funds in Optical Systems by taking equity and thus ensure continuous orders for electronic components.

Both the basic products thus seemed relatively secure.

Financial Management

Finance had been a serious problem for the company from the outset, both in the acquisition of funds to launch the business and in the financial control of operations.

The original agreement reached with the Department of Trade and Industry on the high technology grant under the Support for Innovation Scheme was for one-third of the funds needed to launch the new advanced coordinate measuring equipment. The grant award was contingent on the company raising the remaining two-third portion of the necessary funding, amounting to £40,000 of which Corner himself had managed to provide £15,000 from his own resources. This left £25,000 to be raised from some other source.

A number of banks were approached and eventually an application was made under the Loan Guarantee Scheme for support for this seemingly worthwhile project. Initially Corner was extremely optimistic that the application would be successful and felt that he was receiving encouraging noises from the relevant bank, but the application was eventually turned down. Terry Corner is now somewhat unsure of the reason for refusal; he believes it was because his personal stake in the project was too small – a situation which he sees as being in the classic 'Catch 22' mould.

Industrial and Commercial Finance Corporation (ICFC) were also approached for help and this application also failed, by which time Corner came to the realization that development of his high technology project would have to be postponed – more frustration and a further turning of the 'Catch 22' screw. By this time Corner had begun to refer to himself as 'Major Major' for he further realized that he was now not only ineligible to draw on the innovation grant, but also that the agreement on that grant had a time limit which was rapidly running out. Furthermore he had already won an award for this innovative product and was operating out of rent-free premises in which he was expected to develop it.

Luckily he was able to gain postponement of the deadline for taking up the grant and he was convinced he could generate sufficient funds from his operations in the two basic products to qualify eventually for the grant. In most start-up situations the independent observer would view this belief in early trading surpluses as highly optimistic, particularly in view of the fact that Optical Systems Ltd would necessarily be a one-man operation. Operating on a shoe-string budget on the continuous treadmill of production, record keeping, marketing, negotiating with suppliers and the myriad tedious tasks which all of these functions imply, is unlikely to be the most effective way of generating large cost surpluses. However, Corner reasonably considered that funding would be easier to raise for an established company with a successful trading record than for a new company, so he was not depressed by the postponement.

Cash flow was understandably a major worry at the outset. The £4,000 MIDAS prize money helped but did not last long and Corner still lacked any clear understanding of his finance needs; he also lacked authority in the use of the language of finance which left him at a serious disadvantage in negotiating with banks. Initially he could negotiate only a very small overdraft facility from his bank and this soon proved quite inadequate for his need. Meanwhile, of course, he still had the £15,000 which he had raised specifically for the high technology project and this remained on deposit account, but he was very loath to use any of this for day-to-day operations since he viewed it as his special reserve for eventual funding of his special project. To use it on current operations would have appeared to him as tantamount to an admission of failure of the special project, therefore he was determined to keep this reserve intact.

Initial Operations and Trading Processes

It is useful at this point to describe the relationship Terry Corner developed with the central characters in his trading operations, namely suppliers of components and customers.

Initially his most important customer would be his former employer Derby Optical Company Ltd and it seemed there should be a steady stream of orders for ophthalmic test charts from that source. Corner had departed from Derby Optical Company on very friendly terms. A very cordial relationship together with a high degree of trust still existed between his new company and his former employers.

This special relationship made possible a most unusual deal between the two companies, by which Optical Systems Ltd took over, by way of a kind of informal loan, the stock of the former instruments division of Derby Optical Company. Thus, the new company acquired valuable stock in the form of lenses, mirrors and bodies for profile projectors together with some bodies for ophthalmic test charts on most generous terms. There was a friendly verbal understanding that stock would be paid for as and when sales were realized, either through Derby Optical Company as distributor or direct to the trade. This amounted to a management buy-out on the most generous of deferred payment terms – indeed it was on a sale or return basis – and provided one more good reason for Corner's optimistic view of his company's prospects. As mentioned earlier, Derby Optical Company wished to continue marketing a version of the ophthalmic test chart and was willing to give Corner the option of manufacturing these. It was also agreed that any inquiries received by Derby Optical Company for profile projectors would be routed through Optical Systems Ltd, who were at this stage continuing to receive a fairly steady and healthy stream of inquiries for these products. Corner also believed that plenty more business could be developed in both products by aggressive marketing.

The most expensive component in the range of stocks of raw materials held by Optical Systems Ltd was the electronic control system for the ophthalmic test chart. This component was supplied by a local electronics firm which, we shall call Supplier I, with whom Corner had also established very cordial relations. The proprietor of Supplier I had offered the services of his accounts office to maintain the accounts of Optical Systems Ltd at a nominal charge and Corner had gratefully accepted the offer. At this stage also there was some serious discussion on the possibility of a closer business relationship between the two companies. The proprietor of Supplier I would provide backing for Optical Systems to develop the advanced coordinate measuring equipment in return for a 'stake in the business'. At that time precise details of the financial arrangements were not discussed but undoubtedly some form of equity funding was envisaged by Corner and it was considered that the maintenance of Optical Systems' accounts by Supplier I would provide a basis on which to develop further a relationship that could prove mutually beneficial. In the event, the further relationship did not develop nor did the financial backing materialize; instead, normal trading operations between the two companies soon ran into serious trouble.

Corner had been buying two versions of the electronic component from Supplier I: Mark I comprised a circuit board to which the hand held control unit was connected by cable; Mark II included a more expensive remote control unit. These had been supplied for some considerable time at prices of £95 and £125 respectively. Then in November 1983 Corner was informed by Supplier I that there had been a serious error in their costing of the units and in future the prices would have to be increased to £175 for Mark I and £230 for Mark II.

This news arrived like a bolt from the blue and Corner naturally found it difficult to understand how a well-established business could have made an error of such magnitude and how it could have taken so long to discover the error. Not unreasonably, he reached the conclusion that a unilateral change of policy had taken place as to the terms on which the two companies traded. But what could he do? Their terms of trade had been 'gentlemen's agreements' only and although Corner had placed an order for a large number of electronic components to be supplied at the original price, there was no written commitment from Supplier I to supply at that price; the orders had been placed, as usual, over the telephone and no written confirmation was requested or, indeed, considered necessary. In any case, Corner had no wish to destroy whatever could be salvaged of their relationship by threatening legal acton, which might in any case be a somewhat empty threat, given the slender evidence of agreement he could produce. Besides, Supplier I insisted that a genuine error had occurred.

Meanwhile, he had orders for a large number of ophthalmic charts to be supplied at a fixed contract price – a price which provided a reasonable profit when he could purchase the electronic component at the original cost, but following the cost increase, the contract price would scarcely provide any contribution to overheads. Corner unsuccessfully tried to re-negotiate the selling price with Derby Optical Company who refused because they were convinced the market could not bear the increase. It was obvious that Corner's company could not absorb the extra costs and it would be pointless to do so as he would be working for nothing. Catch 22 was looming large once more – Corner was caught again between an absolute need for performance on the one hand and a complete impossibility of delivery on the other.

It is worth while to introduce the other major sales outlet at this point. Corner had made contact with an independent sales agency in London and arranged for this firm to distribute the ophthalmic test chart on the basis of a 20 per cent sales commission. The relationship with this firm was different from that with the other major business contacts in that it was conducted without any friendship links. Nevertheless, Corner had every faith in the ability of the agency to sell his product and it obviously had incentive to do so. But, as with the other major relationships, there was no written contract binding the two firms together. With the knowledge and cooperation of Supplier I, demonstration units of the various models were provided to the sales agency – Supplier I had earlier demonstrated its faith by providing the electronic components free.

These demonstration units were exhibited at trade fairs with seemingly great success as the feedback was very encouraging. Initial sales through the agency were also running at a reasonable level and Corner was led to believe that prospects were even better, encouraging progress up to the point where the imposition of the increase in the cost of the electronic component threatened to destroy sales completely.

The only possible solution to the dilemma was to find a new supplier of the electronic component at somewhere near the original cost. Corner did in fact find another electronic firm, Supplier II, which was prepared to develop and supply the component at a reasonable price. Using this new component he resumed supply to his distributors as before. Supplier II not only met his price specification but, in Corner's view, provided a superior product.

Meanwhile Supplier I was still operating the accountancy records for Optical Systems Ltd and quickly discovered that sales were continuing although they were not providing the electronic components. The inevitable confrontation which ensued put paid to any lingering friendship in the relationship between the two firms. Supplier I demanded the return of the electronic components which had been supplied on loan for the demonstration units and, in the mêlée which followed, 'diplomatic relations' seem to have been severed.

It was some while later Corner discovered that Supplier I had negotiated directly with the sales agent about the return of its components and during the process of that negotiation had made certain arrangements which had serious implications for the future of Optical Systems Ltd.

Supplier I had determined that it should not lose out on the investment it had made in the development of a circuit board and other equipment for the control unit and, in order to protect its interest, conceived the idea of building the ophthalmic test chart itself and cutting Optical Systems Ltd out of the market. With this objective in mind Supplier I made an arrangement with the same London sales agency, persuading them to dissolve the relationship with Optical Systems Ltd and to become the sole distributer of test charts for Supplier I. At a stroke, Corner found himself divorced from his only contact with the market for his most stable and lucrative product, a most serious blow to his company's prospects.

There was still the opportunity to supply the wooden version of the test chart to Derby Optical Company, but this had never been a very attractive proposition anyway as the profit margin was extremely low. Besides, there had been some debate between the companies about the question of a licensing fee on the test charts; the equipment had been developed while Corner still worked at Derby Optical Company, who now considered that a royalty on sales was due to them. This was an area on which no clear agreement had been reached at the time of setting up operations by Optical Systems Ltd.

The Traumatic Move

By December 1983 conditions in the premises provided by Leicestershire County Council had become unbearable. Low temperatures made working conditions extremely difficult: the size, shape and construction of the building made adequate heating virtually impossible even if Corner could have afforded the heavy costs necessary. The extreme cold caused problems when handling metal objects and working with cold hands created further problems in intricate assembly work.

These difficulties were in themselves sufficient to cause considerable delays in production and to have a serious effect on Corner's productivity, but another result was even more damaging. Rapid heat loss from the corrugated iron building caused dampness and condensation. Overnight cooling of the building encouraged a rapid build up of condensation, resulting in water being deposited on all the machines, mirrors and lenses. Exposed metal parts rusted very quickly but far worse was the effect on the high value lenses. It was essential to dry the lenses, but wiping the surfaces caused staining and smudging which necessitated repolishing of the surfaces, a time-consuming process. Each day hours of valuable time were used up in the depressingly endless process of clearing up.

The depressing nature of these circumstances can, perhaps, be illustrated by analogy to a lone sea voyager whose craft is shipping water and who must spend a large proportion of his day bailing out. In these circumstances the grinding drudgery of ordinary tasks and the time-consuming nature of them demands more energy and willpower than most people are capable of producing. Similarly with the lone small businessman struggling to stay afloat. One can scarcely imagine the effort needed to maintain morale and to regenerate continually the energy required to keep going in this situation. Many small businesses fail if they reach this depressing stage; the aimlessness of the treadmill saps the energy of all but the most indomitable spirit. Paranoia often takes over and objective decision-making becomes impossible. It is natural to lay the blame on others and to become suspicious of business contacts and their motives. That Corner managed to survive through this period is a high compliment to his grit and determination.

Negotiation with the county council landlord did not lead to any satisfactory resolution of the premises problem, although some attempts were made to find a solution. But by this time Corner had determined to return to Derby whatever the economic cost of this further upheaval. He was aware that those costs could be considerable – to leave Leicestershire would almost certainly bring down on him the wrath of his benefactors under the MIDAS award scheme. The proposed departure from Leicestershire would automatically disqualify him from the benefits of the MIDAS scheme, but most of the benefits he had derived from the scheme had already been received and absorbed into his business. The £4,000 prize money had been used as working capital for Optical Systems' current operations, and cash flow was certainly not in such a healthy state that the money could be easily repaid. In fact, it would now begin to appear as if the £4,000 had been misappropriated since it was used for a purpose other than that intended under the award if the competition rules were to be interpreted literally. The free rent benefit had been used for several months and there was the possibility that Leicestershire County Council could demand payment of rent in arrears if disqualification were interpreted literally.

To postpone development of the award-winning idea because of lack of funds could be seen as unfortunate and therefore, regrettable but acceptable; but quitting Leicestershire to set up business elsewhere might well be seen in a rather less favourable light. It was with some trepidation then that Corner announced his intention to pull out of

Leicestershire. He already had enough battles to fight with insufficient troops and if he lost another battle it could mean extinction. In the event, both the MIDAS authorities and Leicestershire County Council were, perhaps, generous in allowing him to go free, though not without a further energy-consuming skirmish.

After release from Shepshed, Optical Systems Ltd was soon set up in suitable premises in Derby. The move did involve some costs. There was the immediate cost in time and expense of the removal itself and the need to begin paying rent immediately. But against these costs can be set the benefits of convenience and, above all, suitability of premises.

For Optical Systems Ltd re-establishing in Derby meant virtually starting all over again. Most of their previous market in ophthalmic test charts had been lost in the unfortunate circumstances described, and in the desparate days at the Shepshed works it was quite impossible to impress a prospective client in the profile projector market, so that most of the business had been lost in that area also.

What Went Wrong?

It may be useful at this point to consider some of the possible reasons for the inability to get the business moving.

First, there is clearly the possibility that the venture was always too risky to have a reasonable chance of success. The fact that Derby Optical Company, with its long experience, felt unable to operate profitably in this market might suggest that there was no reasonable chance of success for a novice. But there are many examples of successful management buy-outs following the decision of a large company management to pull out because the operation was unattractive (indeed, we have given one in the previous chapter). It is, therefore, not reasonable to suggest that the operation had no chance of success whatever the circumstances and we must look closely at other reasons for the slow start.

The lack of adequate funding was a serious disadvantage from the outset. As we have argued in chapter 1, this is not an unusual problem in new businesses; it is very common even among those which eventually succeed, but it makes life extremely difficult. The lack of understanding of financial needs not only leads to questionable decision-making but also presents a totally unconvincing picture to financial institutions and consequently makes the raising of funds much more difficult. The bank manager feels most at ease with those who can speak his language and he will more readily lend to them.

There is a further, perhaps even more damaging lack of business sophistication from which Terry Corner has suffered – general communication skills. He is a highly intelligent person capable of adapting quickly in difficult situations but his lack of sophisticated knowledge in his chosen scientific technological field puts him at serious disadvantage and may make clear communication with prospective backers and clients very difficult, leaving a credibility gap in the eyes of the client.

The fact that the business is a one-man operation tends to exaggerate this credibility gap in a high technology market. 'What if he is unable to deliver to specification?' 'How will he manage to provide the back-up of an after-sales service when he must always look after the shop?' These questions are bound to arise in the minds of prospective clients, almost all of whom will be employees of large organizations and accustomed to operating what they would consider to be a more secure and efficient system. Security is important to them; they are risk-averse and Optical Systems Ltd looks like very high risk.

This problem loops back to the old vicious circle of Corner's inability to be convincing until his firm is well established but it cannot be established until it can present a convincing face. This leads to the question of whether it is technically feasible to have a successful one-man production operation in a high technology field.

Again, good legal advice before launching the new business might have avoided many of the problems and disputes in which Corner fared badly because he had neither the time nor the legal expertise to handle them well. Accepting informal agreements as a basis for a business operation may seem like indefensible naivety on the part of any businessman, but it is not unusual for small businesses to have informal agreements with both suppliers and customers. Perhaps what is unusual in this case is that there were so many informalities and that they were so central to the company's operations and, consequently, so important to its survival. When setting up business on a shoestring however (and one suspects that most small operations are), legal advice on such niceties as licensing agreements and supply contracts can easily be seen as an unnecessary expense and cause of delay.

The failure of the informal agreements was due partly to lack of understanding and clear communication between the parties to them, but failure was probably inevitable given the imprecise nature of the agreements from the beginning. Good technical advice could surely have avoided some of these damaging failures.

Finally, it is reasonable to ask also whether winning an award in the MIDAS competition was any advantage to Terry Corner? The 'traumatic move' to a strange environment may have brought its own problems – being away from his own familiar territory, divorced from helpful contacts, is often considered to provide serious problems for new business starters, particularly in highly technical operations and even more particularly when the starter is unsophisticated in the ways of business. Corner himself dismisses the 'away from home' problem as unimportant but stresses the difficulties caused by having to work in unsuitable premises, and undoubtedly the depressing conditions of the Shepshed building were a contributory factor in the loss of business sustained at the time. As we noted in chapter 1 this is a potential problem for all business competition winners; in their keenness to get started, they may be tempted to accept unsuitable premises and later discover they have won more problems than benefits.

The authors' experience with prize-winners suggests that many of the winners would derive more benefit from good advice than from prize money. Sympathetic consultancy is essential in these circumstances: it is not sufficient to advise winners that they can have free consultancy if they ask for it.

Many new entrepreneurs do not have the ability to recognize their problems or to articulate them clearly; nor do they have the time to seek consultancy advice – the treadmill syndrome again. To be useful in this situation a consultant must have a clear knowledge of the general difficulties of small business managers and must be capable of leading the manger gently to a recognition of the main problem areas in his own business. It may be that this is the area where small business competitions can provide most help in the future.

The Future

The future prospects for Optical Systems Ltd look somewhat bleak at this time. The basic activities of the business have not been going well and the high technology project has failed to take off, though it has not been abandoned – merely postponed. Funding of that special project continues to be a major problem, although we believe there are some possible sources which have not been thoroughly explored as yet. For example, various local businesses have expressed an interest in providing some backing for the project but so far these have come to naught, partly because of Terry Corner's own reticence. He believes that prospective equity partners want too much for the money they are prepared to put up; that is they want a larger share of the business than he is prepared to concede.

This suspicion on his part may be partly due to his unfortunate and costly previous experience with prospective partners, but it is also symptomatic of a disease common among many inventive entrepreneurs – they have a phobia about losing their 'creation'. They will often take a very dim view of a prospective backer who demands 40 per cent of the equity in return for putting up the funds needed to launch the idea, forgetting that this is very high risk funding and that, consequently, the backer is not unreasonable in demanding a large share of the possible returns. They forget also that it is much better to own 60 per cent of a thriving business than 100 per cent of a good idea which may never be converted into business. Moreover, it seems remarkable how fiercely entrepreneurs resist the whole idea of allowing outside equity participation at the time of start-up, but at the same time, can look forward eagerly to a future when they may be in a position to have the company's shares quoted on the Stock Exchange Unlisted Securities Market (USM). No doubt they believe that they can demand a much higher price for equity participation once the company is sufficiently established to qualify for the USM, but it does imply a willingness to relinquish some equity, so there is a logical inconsistency in that attitude. Besides, relinquishing equity at the outset may be the best way, indeed the only way, to raise funds for many high technology (and high risk) projects.

Corner believes his company will qualify for the high technology grant whenever he can raise the extra funding, but it seems unlikely that the Department of Trade and Industry could have agreed to a postponement of the project *sine die*. Since the first application was successful, there is probably a good chance that a new application, submitted within a reasonable time, will receive sympathetic treatment, but there is always a danger that Optical Systems's scheme may be technologically dated and unworthy of support.

Raising the remainder of the required funds still poses the greatest difficulty for Optical Systems Ltd. At present it seems very unlikely that the existing business can generate enough surplus to fill the gap; that possibility is remote at this stage owing to the problems outlined in this chapter. We have not claimed that any of these problems is unusual in new businesses, indeed many small businesses suffer them at one time or another, but it is, fortunately, rare to suffer them all at once or over such a short period of time.

Terry Corner seems to have suffered more than his fair share of ill luck, but now he only needs a little good fortune to start winning. A few good orders for profile projectors could provide some margin for further development and the idea which won the MIDAS award is still a good idea even if it has not yet got past the prototype stage. Corner still has enough energy, enthusiasm and dogged determination to make it work, and these qualities, perhaps more than any other, are the basis of successful entrepreneurial effort.

6 The Challenge of an Elusive Market

This is a story of Sycon Products. It is the story of an inventor–entrepreneur with two good products that common sense, right reason and favourable ratings all suggest a lot of people need. The problem has been to convince these people that they want them, and want them enough to pay the asking price. This chapter explores this paradox.

At the same time, the story of Sycon Products introduces other themes. We have a close-up of an entrepreneur's initial production problems; they are small problems, but this is invariably the case, and their solution still takes time and energy. We have an entrepreneur with long experience in family business, and complicated connections between his new and old business concerns. We see high-minded responsibility to employees and a sense of family obligation affect the timing and content of business moves. The imponderable of pricing new products for which there is no established market, and the relation between price and market strategy form compelling sub-plots to the main story. Anyone who thinks there cannot really be that much to selling a new product should ask themselves two questions: first, could they have devised the marketing initiatives this entrepreneur has already executed; and second, what would they do next?

Background History

In 1981 an established Leicestershire firm, H. Roberts &

Brooks (Syston) Limited, secured an order from the Dr Barnardo's charity for the design and manufacture of a set of minibus steps capable of being fitted over a tow bar. In the same year the theft of a trailer from the premises of Roberts & Brooks prompted the owner of the company, Bryan Roberts, to start work on designing an anti-theft parker post for trailers. Prototypes of both these products, tow bar steps and the trailer parker system, were completed approximately a year later, in August 1982. At the time Bryan Roberts entered the MIDAS competition (the Spring of 1983) both products were on the verge of being marketed as Sycon Products. His MIDAS submission covered both products, but only the trailer parker system was selected for an award.

H. Roberts & Brooks (Syston) Ltd. was founded by Bryan Roberts's father in association with a partner in 1934. The company traded as a road haulage concern until 1946 when it was converted to a garage. Mr. Roberts senior bought out his partner in 1960, from which time the company has been owned by the Roberts family. Bryan enjoyed a successful career in industry prior to joining his family's company in 1968 at the age of 34. Having served a six-year apprenticeship in the motor trade and undertaken a diploma course in production engineering, he became a management trainee with a major chemical company. During his time with this company he specialized in the petro-chemical side of the business, designing and selling exothermic stress relieving kits both at home and abroad. Personal reasons concerned with his father's health resulted in him taking over the family business in 1968.

Bryan Roberts had only limited interest and enthusiasm for the garage business and within a year had opened a motorists' discount shop, one of the first in the country. The success of this venture enabled him to expand the business rapidly in the early 1970s. A new shop was built to the side of the garage and a new garage built at the rear of the premises (an increased amount of fleet maintenance work necessitated the building of a larger garage). The original garage was converted to another shop, specializing in leisure and camping goods.

Both the turnover and profits of the company increased

steadily during the 1970s. By 1978 the turnover of the company had risen from £30,000 in 1968 to approximately £½ million per annum. Staff during the same period increased from two to 16 and new staff facilities and offices were in the process of being constructed above the motorists shop. The discount motorists' shop was, however, the main contributor to growth during this period. The camping and leisure side of the business was facing declining sales by 1978 and was closed. A sports shop run by Bryan Roberts's daughter was opened in its place. It was also becoming apparent by 1978 that revenue from the motorists' shop was under serious threat. The economic environment had become increasingly hostile due to the emergence of national chains of such shops in the seventies. While the garage side of the business continued to function profitably, local trade had considerably declined since the garage had been moved to the rear of the premises. Many local people thought that the garage had been closed.

Confronted by the problem of the likely decline in the motorist shop trade Bryan Roberts looked for new areas of growth. He developed a new side to the business – trailer hire and sales. Although the company had previously sold camping trailers and related accessories, for example tow bar fittings, this new venture greatly expanded its involvement in this area. The company not only sold and hired out standard trailers but also designed and constructed or converted trailers for specialized purposes. This new venture resulted in greater utilization of the garage space and enabled Bryan Roberts to exploit more fully his personal interest and training in engineering. By 1981 the trailer centre business formed the major part of the company's operations and it was this new business that gave rise to Sycon Products.

The Decision to Develop

The two new products to be marketed by Sycon Products were not developed with a view to diversifying the company's activities. As already noted, the trailer parker system was developed for the company's own security purposes and the tow bar steps were initially regarded as simply a one-off order. Also the company had no manufacturing facilities capable of producing the components for either product. The manufacture of the components for the prototypes was sub-contracted to local firms. Why then was a decision taken to market these products?

Various factors related to the position of the company in 1982 and the nature of the products themselves influenced Bryan Roberts's decision to market them.

By 1982 the anticipated decline in the motorist shop's trade had been fully realized. Stocks were being run down with a view to eventually phasing out this business. The marriage of Roberts's daughter necessitated the closing of the sports shop. While it had been capable of providing a reasonable living to a member of his family, it was not sufficiently profitable to justify the appointment of a full-time manager. The garage trade had also continued to decline between 1978 and 1982. Although the turnover of the business had declined from its 1978 peak, the business as a whole continued to be a profitable concern due to the trailer centre. The problem confronting Bryan Roberts at the start of 1982 was essentially what to do with the considerable space that was becoming available due to the closure of the shops. If the company was to continue to operate from its existing premises, new areas of business needed to be developed. Since both his own and his parents' house were located on the business premises, Roberts felt under considerable pressure at this time to expand into new areas. The decision to market Sycon products was taken partly as a result of this pressure.

A number of factors concerning the products themselves, however, were decisive in terms of taking the decision to develop them. First, the effort and time that was devoted to their design and the manufacture of prototypes. When the projects were started Roberts considered that both would take a matter of weeks to design and produce; in the event they took almost a year. Secondly, it became apparent once the prototypes were produced that both products were completely original and capable of being patented. The only question that remained to be answered prior to marketing was 'did a market for them exist?'.

From the time the prototypes were produced Roberts was convinced there was a market for the products, particularly the trailer parker system. Through operating the trailer centre he was already aware of the large number of thefts of trailer vehicles of all sorts, including caravans. In selling trailers he had encountered situations when potential customers were deterred by the fear that they were too easily stolen. Also once the prototypes had been installed on the company's premises customers expressed considerable interest in purchasing the system.

Roberts' confidence in the market potential of the trailer parker system was reinforced when it was selected for a MIDAS award. The only market research he undertook for his MIDAS application was to determine the total number of trailer units, private, commercial and industrial, in the UK. A mere 2.5 per cent of this market, 50,000 units, represented a potential turnover of approximately £2 million. In addition, it was estimated that the European trailer market was at least twice that of the UK. In the light of this, Roberts budgeted a modest 5,000 units (£133,000) sales in the first year of operations, rising to 50,000 units by the third year.

From the launch of the trailer parker system in April 1983 to the end point of this study, only 150 units were sold. The production and marketing of the product created a serious financial crisis which almost destroyed the whole company in December 1983. Given the optimism about the product's future displayed by both Bryan Roberts and the MIDAS panel, what went wrong?

The Trailer System

Design and Production

In developing the trailer system for his own use, Bryan Roberts was concerned about two essential design features – stability and security. The system had to be capable of providing level and stable support for a trailer while at the same time ensuring its security. Although the design took nine months, the product is very simple. It consists of a main post on to which is welded a lock bar and a small horizontal plate carrying a standard size 50 mm ball. Above it is a sliding top plate which when padlocked in position prevents the trailer coupling being released from the ball (see figure 6.1). The system can be used either simply as a parking post or as a security post if the top plate and a padlock are in place.

While the prototypes produced in August 1982 met his own requirements, Roberts regarded them as deficient as saleable products in two respects – versatility and finish. He considered the system needed to be more acceptable to various situations with respect to how and where the post

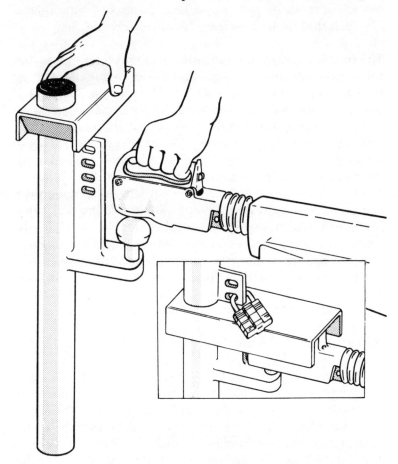

Figure 6.1   The Sycon Products lockable trailer parker system.

was to be secured. Between August and November he designed a range of models to overcome this problem.

The range of five models decided upon comprised the following:

- basic model – post cemented directly into the ground;
- popular model – post located into a socket which is cemented into the ground;
- wall model – post bolted directly on to a wall;
- surface model – post slides into a retaining plate which is bolted to concrete;
- screw model – post has a large corkscrew type thread such that it can be screwed into soft ground.

The problem concerning the finish of the prototypes was that they had been electroplated and hence required painting with zinc-rich paint once installed. To avoid the necessity of painting Roberts decided to have the posts galvanized.

The first production order was placed in February 1983. Roberts's previous business experience enabled him easily to identify potential suppliers and obtain quotes. Production involved sub-contracting the manufacture of the system to three different organizations. Pre-cut lengths of tubing for the posts were delivered direct to Roberts & Brooks or to a local firm which hole-punched those to be used in the 'popular' model. An order for the sub-assemblies comprising lock bar, ball and bottom plates was placed with another local firm. This firm manufactured the tooling for the sub-assemblies and manufactured, welded and case-hardened the sub-assemblies; it also manufactured the top plates. The welding of the sub-assembly into the post was done at Roberts & Brooks before the completed product was sent to a third firm for galvanizing.

The trailer system was launched via a direct marketing campaign in April 1983. Production problems, however, resulted in there being not a single item in stock at the start of the campaign. Delays in the manufacture of the tooling required for the sub-assemblies resulted in the first batch of a thousand being delivered in June. In addition, the first batch of 50 completed units received from the galvanizing firm had an unacceptable finish. In order to produce an acceptable finish the posts needed to be spun during the galvanizing process. Roberts discovered only two Midland firms capable of undertaking this work and transferred the galvanizing process to a Birmingham firm. The spinning process produced the desired results but created additional problems. The posts were subjected to higher treatment temperatures during the spinning process which caused structural changes in the surface of the metal, destroying the case-hardening. In July 1983 Roberts decided to return to electroplating and had a leaflet produced recommending the customer to paint the post with zinc-rich paint. The leaflet accompanied delivery of the product.

One of the first sales of the trailer system resulted in a customer complaint and the discovery of a design flaw. The lock bars had been designed with three holes punched in them. The three-hole lock bar failed to accommodate certain older makes of caravan, such that the top plate could not be secured. A five-hole lock bar was needed to secure these older models. The three-hole lock bars had to be burned off the first batch of sub-assemblies at a cost of £2,000 in terms of lost production.

These were problems encountered early on, but they took their toll. Bryan Roberts is now satisfied with the current production arrangements. He has no particular desire to bring production in-house. The current production lead time of approximately 12 weeks is unlikely to present problems unless demand goes well in excess of 5,000 units per annum. In the event of the producer of the sub-assemblies being unable to meet production needs, production of the sub-assemblies could easily be transferred to another company; Roberts & Brooks paid for and owns the tooling for these components.

Bryan Roberts blames himself for the early production problems. In retrospect he recognizes that he paid insufficient attention to both design detail and production. Before perfecting a single model he had already moved on to extending the range of products. His interest, he feels, lies too much on the engineering and innovation side of products rather than their marketing. In the case of the trailer system, however, he attributes part of the early production problems simply to being in too much of a rush. By the time the product was marketed in 1983 he was feeling under considerable pressure to get a new side to the business off the ground. The pressure was not so much financial, as a feeling of responsibility towards his workforce. He found it very difficult to lay off his employees as the garage business and shops declined and saw the Sycon products as a way of halting, if not reversing, this trend.

Marketing the Trailer System

In his MIDAS application Bryan Roberts identified three market segments for his trailer system:

- private: owners of caravans, trailers, boat trailers, etc.;
- commercial: retailers of caravans, trailers, boats, etc. and operators of caravan sites and marinas;
- industrial/local authority: industrial concerns using trailer equipment, compressors, welders, generators, etc.

It was decided that the initial sales effort should be directed towards the private segment; this market provided the largest profit margin for the company. Over the winter months of 1982 £7,000 was spent on designing and printing promotional material for Sycon Products and a direct marketing campaign costing £5,000 was launched in April 1983.

The marketing campaign which covered the period April to August 1983 involved advertising in leisure magazines concerned with caravanning and boating. The advertisements briefly outlined the trailer system, emphasizing the security aspect, and required the potential customer to send off for further details. An order form was then sent with the promotional material. This approach was adopted on the basis that Roberts considered it most unlikely customers would pay in excess of £40 for a product for which there was no established market.

The direct marketing campaign resulted in sales of 29

units. Roberts attributed the failure of this campaign to two aspects: first, the protracted nature of the ordering process; secondly, the fact that the product received no additional publicity via the product review sections of the magazines. However, when full page product reviews were devoted to the trailer system in spring 1984 in *Caravanning* monthly and in *Camping and Caravanning*, few inquiries resulted, even though one reviewer concluded: 'The Sycon system is particularly easy to install and to use; it is well presented with easy-to-follow instructions, and it is very strongly made. We rate it very highly.' Similar sentiments were expressed by the other reviewer.

The failure of the direct marketing campaign persuaded Roberts in August 1983 to turn his attention towards the commercial sector. Attempts were made to sell to caravan stockists using a mail shot and through trade shows. In addition, a mail shot was made to hoteliers operating establishments near to the sea, lakes and the Norfolk Broads with a view to trying to get them to instal the system for the convenience of their boat-owning clients. While considerable interest and enthusiasm for the product was expressed by caravan retailers at trade shows, the trade shows and mail shot combined resulted in only a dozen stockists. Each stockist took only two or three posts. No inquiries resulted from the mail shot to hoteliers.

Two new approaches to trying to reach the private customer were developed in 1984. An arrangement was made for promotion of the product with an insurance company specializing in caravan insurance. The insurance company agreed to endorse the product and send out with its renewal policies promotional material about the Sycon system, encouraging their clients to purchase it. The system was offered at a special promotion price, including a free insurance padlock. In its first two months the promotion resulted in six orders.

A second new sales initiative was directed towards trying to get a caravan site owner to adopt and promote the system. At the time of writing discussions were taking place with the owners of a site where more than 200 caravans are permanently located. The owners were considering installing the sockets and selling the posts to their customers, again at a special promotional price. The attraction of the Sycon system from the site owner's viewpoint was not only its security aspect but also its versatility. In order to maintain the site the caravan owners must regularly re-site their caravans. A small modification to the design of the socket of the Sycon system would enable owners to rotate their caravans a full 360° around the post, thus minimizing the disruption caused by re-siting. Roberts believed that the establishment of the Sycon trailer system in one site would greatly increase the chances of its adoption elsewhere. Further approaches were also being made to the owners of caravan sites and marinas.

A new approach was also adopted latterly to commercial sales. An agreement was reached with an organization supplying retailers whereby the parker system would be included in their catalogue but orders would be handled directly by Roberts & Brooks.

Finally, a number of new sales initiatives were considered. Roberts set out to tap the industrial/local authority market by exhibiting at a major public works exhibition in November 1984. He also contacted house builders with a view to persuading them to install the system on the premises of new homes. Bryan Roberts also set about writing a pamphlet on caravan handling which he intended to sell through caravan retailers. The pamphlet was to deal with a range of problems concerned with caravan ownership, focusing on the merits of the Sycon system for manoeuvring and securing caravans.

The Failure to Sell

The trailer parker system was selected for a MIDAS award, the product received enthusiastic product reviews and roused considerable interest when exhibited at trade shows, but it did not sell. Why? Was it primarily, as Bryan Roberts believes, due to his failure to survey the market properly and successfully sell the concept of the system, or did other factors create the main barrier to sales?

It is certainly true that Roberts failed to survey the market. No attempt was made to establish what the consumer or the trade wanted from such a system or the price they would be willing to pay. Roberts now considers he has been asking people to buy a product they do not understand or fully appreciate. The versatility of the system, he feels, has been overlooked and he thinks people are always reluctant to spend money on security. For a long time he believed the price of the system, at £43.50, was about right, but he now admits that such a view was founded on the fact that nobody suggested to him it was the price that deterred them from purchase.

There can be little doubt that the pricing of a new product for which there is no established market is a very hit-and-miss affair. Roberts calculated a standard cost for the various models based on 5,000 budgeted units and then added what he considered a reasonable profit margin. The costing system reflected Roberts's inexperience in the area of finance and resulted, partly intentionally, in a very conservative cost, that is, a high cost. Overhead recovery rates were based on the first year's budgeted sales, a figure established by reference to trying to minimize postage costs in the dispatch of ordered units even though overhead costs were expected to be the same at 15,000 units of production.

In addition, the identification of overheads was approached in a conservative manner. Items were included to be 'on the safe side' and the allocation of the overheads relating to the premises further reflected this tendency towards conservatism. In essence, a rudimentary cost-plus pricing system was developed.

Bryan Roberts appreciated that certain aspects of his costings would result in the product being priced on the high side. He was, however, not unhappy about this strategy on the basis, he believes, it is always easier to reduce prices than raise them. The marketing strategy he adopted was essentially a top of the market one involving skimming at high prices.

Winkler identifies a number of factors associated with the use of this strategy, including: there being no comparable competition, new product innovation, little danger of competitor entry due to patent control, high research and development (R & D) costs and high promotion costs, and inelastic demand.[1] He also identifies the main disadvantage of the strategy as being that it 'assumes that a market exists at high prices' and he states that the procedure for adopting the strategy should include determining preliminary customer reaction. While a number of Winkler's factors concerning the use of the skimming strategy are applicable to the trailer parker system, no attempt was made to test the market; it could be that a market for the system simply does not exist at the current price level.

An alternative for Roberts would have been to pursue a market-related approach to pricing and possibly a down-market, market penetration strategy for sales. Such an approach to pricing would have involved, *inter alia*, research into how much the various market segments he identified would bear in terms of price and the establishment of cost and profit objectives in the light of this information. A down-market sales strategy would have involved trying to stimulate market growth and create a mass market for the product through low prices. An obvious market segment for this approach would be the commercial sector, in particular caravan and marina site owners. Roberts is convinced that if private trailer owners were familiarized with the benefits of the system, sales to that segment would expand rapidly. Familiarization via caravan sites is now part of Roberts's current sales strategy.

To a large extent one may regard the pricing policy and market strategy adopted by Bryan Roberts as being forced upon him. The pressure he felt under 'to get the product to the market as quickly as possible' coupled with the fact that Sycon Products is essentially a one-man business, limited his options. He had neither the time nor the experience to engage in market research. What really excites him is the development of new products, not marketing them. Although he has countenanced the idea of a partner to look after the commercial side of his business, he prefers the idea of 'going it alone', a tendency very strong among inventor–entrepreneurs, as was argued in chapter 5. There can, however, be little doubt that in managing the whole business alone he has been unable to devote sufficient time to the promotion of Sycon Products. He now recognizes that mail order is not the right medium through which to sell a new and unfamiliar product; he needs to go out and sell the concept of the trailer parker system. He has also become more aware of the importance of trying to establish the price sensitivity of demand for the product, and is currently restructuring his prices with a view to testing it.

The Tow Bar Steps

The tow bar steps developed for Dr Barnardo's were designed to be fitted directly to tow bars being used on rear-entry minibuses. The design involved two steps, one above and one below the tow bar, with the top step folding down to reveal the towing attachment. In designing the steps a great deal of attention was paid to the safety aspect. The steps were designed to ensure there would be no risk of injury to users through catching their feet or legs on the towing attachment when entering or leaving a vehicle. The safety aspect figured prominently in the promotional material for the steps and reflected Bryan Roberts's view that the main potential customers for the steps would be educational authorities and social services. Sales in the private sector to organizations such as schools, old peoples' homes and scout groups were also considered a possibility.

Although the steps and the promotional material relating to them were developed in parallel with the trailer parker system, their marketing took second place. From the outset Roberts regarded the steps as having a more limited market potential. In addition, the MIDAS award, coupled with the fact that caravanning is a seasonal activity, encouraged Roberts to devote all of his energies in the spring of 1983 towards marketing the trailer parker system.

Prototypes of the steps were produced in August 1982. As with the trailer parker system, production of components was sub-contracted to local firms and only assembly and packing undertaken at Roberts & Brooks. The company also offered a fitting service to local customers. Unlike the trailer parker system no problems were encountered in production and the ten prototypes constituted saleable units. No attempt was made to market the steps for a year but the original batch of ten were sold during this period mainly as a result of Roberts's personal contacts. Five sets were sold to Leicestershire Education Authority.

Bryan Roberts turned his attention to marketing the steps following the failure of the direct marketing campaign for the trailer parker system. Fifty sets of steps were manufactured in August 1983 and a mail shot was directed at county councils. Only ten sales resulted. In October social services transport officers throughout the country were identified by telephone and a second mail shot was directed at named individuals. A further 20 sales resulted. The remaining 20 units from the production batch of 50 were sold through trade shows and advertisements in local government magazines.

Although only 60 sets of steps had been sold by August 1984, at that time Roberts was more optimistic about this product than the trailer parker system. He believed it could well be the first to 'take off'. This optimism was founded on the response he received from exhibiting at trade shows. Representatives from both the police and the fire services were expressing considerable interest in the product but Roberts considered the main problem of selling to these organizations, and more generally to commercial and industrial organizations, was the price. The high price of the steps, £100, was to a large extent attributed to the fact that they were 'over-engineered'. At the end point of our study promotion of the steps has been suspended pending the production of a simplified one-step model which it was anticipated would be priced between £40 and £50.

In retrospect Bryan Roberts considers he miscalculated the potential market for this product. In devoting so much time to the safety aspect in designing the steps he automatically thought that the main market for the product would be on vehicles transporting either the old or the young. He was also aware that selling in this market would prove difficult. The steps afforded minibus users the opportunity to tow trailers, but Roberts was confronted with the problem of convincing the user of the benefits of this additional facility. What he tended to overlook was the market where the user already had a tow bar attachment but either no steps or unsafe steps. The main market in this area comprises fleet operators such as the gas board, electricity board, building contractors etc. It is this market to which Roberts is now turning his attention. Fleet owners operating vehicles with tow bar attachments have been identified and he intends launching a sales campaign at these and minibus suppliers featuring the cheaper model of the steps.

The Costs of Failure

Excluding the cost of Bryan Roberts's time in designing Sycon Products, the designing, patenting, production and marketing of the products has involved an investment of around £50,000; little of this investment has yet been recouped via sales revenue. This expenditure coincided with declining revenue from all but the trailer centre side of Roberts & Brooks' business and has been funded by bank overdraft. The premises of Roberts & Brooks have been heavily under utilized for the past two years, and have been a major drain on the cash resources of the business. With only storage, assembly and packing of the Sycon Products being undertaken at Roberts & Brooks, Sycon's activities have not resulted in utilization of the space freed by closure of the sports shop and run-down and eventual closure of the motorist shop in 1984. In addition, the garage is well in excess of the size required to justify the current level of work.

Bryan Roberts was not prepared for the cash flow implications of the two Sycon products failing to sell. The first cash flow forecast he prepared was for his MIDAS entry and he did not realize, and nobody pointed out to him, the implications of it if things did not go according to plan. In the winter of 1983 the company suffered a severe cash flow crisis, with the bank pressing for Roberts to reduce the company's overdraft. Roberts reflects on the latter months of 1983 as a time during which he 'experienced immense strain'. He is a local businessman who feels a strong sense of responsibility towards the local community, in particular his workforce. As the business declined in 1982 he had found it difficult to lay off members of his workforce, some of whom had worked for the company for many years, and in December 1983 the cash crisis necessitated further painful decisions in this area.

The personal costs to Bryan Roberts during this troubled period were high. Not only did he 'lose sleep' over the decisions he was forced to take to save the business, but it seriously undermined for a time his confidence in his own ability to take rational business decisions. Even though he had built an extremely successful business in the seventies, he started to question whether he had really run the business as efficiently as he could have during those years. His confidence in 'professionals' was also undermined. While appreciating the bank's position, at the same time he felt 'let down' by the suddenness of the actions which prompted the cash crisis.

The stringent cash constraints under which the company operated after December 1983 obviously limited the scope for expenditure on marketing Sycon's products. Nevertheless, having taken the necessary decisions to bring the company's cash flow under control, involving closing the motorists' shop, Bryan Roberts regained much of his confidence in himself and the business and he is now optimistic about the future of Sycon Products.

The Way Forward

A great deal of uncertainty still surrounds the future of Sycon Products. When we last visited Bryan Roberts he had taken a decision on a matter which he considered had long been an impediment to ensuring the success of the products. He was in the process of drawing up plans for the disposal of a substantial part of the premises of Roberts & Brooks, retaining only sufficient space from which to operate the trailer centre and Sycon Products.

For some considerable time the premises were an encumbrance rather than an asset to the successful operation of the company. Roberts postponed the decision concerning the premises partly because initially he could see no way, given their situation, of retaining only sufficient for his needs and partly because of the implications for his workforce. In delaying the decision not only did he distract himself from devoting sufficient time and effort to his new products, but also he helped create the cash flow problems of 1983. The major lesson he learned from his experiences was the need to 'clear the books' before beginning on a major new scheme. Had he rationalized the business earlier and sold part of the premises, then it would have released funding for the new product, reduced or eliminated the pressure on him to rush the products to the market and allowed him to devote considerably more time to the problem of trying to establish a market for the new products.

The lessons learned by Sycon Products can be grouped under three broad headings: engineering and production, marketing, and finance.

Engineering and Production

Bryan Roberts started his working life as an engineer and with little effort successfully transferred to being a shop-keeper. In developing Sycon Products he reverted to his real interest, engineering, but he has found the transition from engineer to entrepreneur a difficult one.

As an engineer he rightly prides himself on having designed products that met the requirements he was particularly concerned with: security in the case of the trailer parker system and safety in terms of the steps. He recognizes however that in focusing so strongly on these aspects, both products were 'over-engineered'. In addition, the promotional material for the products was too conditioned by the attention he paid to these aspects in designing the products. The engineer needs to step back from his products and in marketing them consider the range of benefits that the products he has developed afford the customer. In doing so he may more easily identify the potential market segments for the products.

Bryan Roberts considers that he needs to curb his enthusiasm for the engineering side of the business if he is to be successful. Rather than designing and producing a single product and ensuring it is satisfactory in every detail, he has a tendency to rush into designing new models or variations without really considering their market potential; for example, the screw model of the trailer parker system which has not sold at all. His enthusiasm for engineering he feels also permeates his approach to marketing – he tends to be too technical when he promotes his products.

Marketing

Marketing, like any other aspect of a business, requires careful planning. The approach adopted for marketing the Sycon products was rushed and haphazard. Roberts now appreciates the need thoroughly to research and test his markets, decide a strategy for each market segment and carefully schedule the launch of products. He also sees the need to feed back the marketing information into his business plan in terms of setting profit and cost objectives. It is doubtful with the current resources available to the company, financially and in terms of manpower, whether he could accomplish all he may wish to in this area, but at least he is now more aware of the pitfalls.

Finance

Finance is an area in which Bryan Roberts concedes he could well do with professional help and advice. The problem is cost. The firm is audited by a major firm of chartered accountants and he therefore knows how expensive professional advice can be. In retrospect he is somewhat surprised that the MIDAS panel did not scrutinize and question either his projected cash flow or his costings. The cash flow crisis of 1983 brought home to him the importance of establishing from the outset how much capital would be required and ensuring that it would be available. He sympathizes with those who have to start from scratch; he is sure that he would not have been able to support Sycon Products for so long had it not been for his trailer centre business.

Sycon Products may yet become a household name to caravanning and boating enthusiasts as Bryan Roberts desires. Just as a week is a long time in politics so it is in business; a breakthrough may not be far away.

Note

1 J. Winkler, *Pricing for Results* (Heinemann, London, 1983).

7 Raising Finance and Cash Constraints

In this chapter we consider the problems some of the businesses we looked at had in raising finance, their experiences in tackling those problems, and the effects these problems had on the way the businesses were run. We have deliberately not discussed finance until this point in the book as we believe the points made will be more will be more interesting and more meaningful coming after several practical case histories.

Understandably, most of our sample of companies would not wish to see full details of their personal financial situation published. We have also found with small firms in general that in some cases they give a rather more favourable impression of their financial position than could really be justified on referring to their accounts. We are not therefore going to present a detailed numerical analysis of the financial position of the companies in our sample, but instead illustrate some impressions and propositions with specific examples, some drawn from our wider experience. We have also, in most cases, not named the businesses from whom we draw our examples.

Why a Business needs Money

A newly launched business needs finance for three broad purposes:

- *Investment in tangible, fixed assets*. These are the assets bought for use in the business such as machinery, plant, fixtures and fittings and motor vehicles. The business premises might also fall in this category, but most of the businesses in our sample chose to rent rather than buy property.

– *Intangible investment*. This broad heading covers the costs of setting up and developing a business which are not represented by tangible assets. Examples might include the costs of developing a new product, market research, advertising and staff training costs. Normal accounting practice is to regard such costs as expenses of the year in which they arise. However, in a new or developing business the economic reality of the situation is that these costs represent an investment in the future, creating the 'goodwill' of the business.

– *Working capital*. This is a term used to describe the finance tied up in those items which form part of the operating cycle of the business. The operating cycle of a simple business might be as follows:

– suppliers send the business stock in the sense of raw materials or components on credit terms;

– stock is sold to customers, on credit terms, so that the customers become 'debtors' of the business;

– in due course (typically after 30 – 60 days) debtors pay cash;

– cash is paid to creditors.

Any increase in the level of business activity initially involves more finance being tied up in stock and debtors; it is only over a period of time that the additional profit on trading produces sufficient cash inflow to cover this cash outlay.

Owners' Personal Investment

Financial resources put into the business by the owners, often referred to as the 'equity' in the business, are an essential source of finance. Lenders are understandably reluctant to put money into a business unless the proprietors are also investing a significant amount of their own money.

There are two reasons for this. First, in the event of a business being unsuccessful, and making losses, lenders will want to be confident that these losses will be covered by the proprietors' own share of the business and that the business will still be able to repay the loans. Second, if the proprietors have a substantial personal financial commitment they will be more likely to be both cautious and hard working in their management of the business.

Where the personal financial resources of the entrepreneur are insufficient to provide a significant amount of equity, it is possible to invite other people to invest in the equity of the business as co-owners. However, in practice the owners of a small, newly launched business are likely to find this course of action both difficult and undesirable for the following reasons:

- *The Stock Exchange*, which offers facilities to bring companies and investors together, is in practice very costly to approach. As a source of finance it is out of the question for small businesses.
- *Profits of the business* will have to be shared among a greater number of owners. The entrepreneur who has the original business idea will be reluctant to share the benefits with other investors.
- *The entrepreneur* is likely to be reluctant to share control with other investors, particularly if left with only a minority share.
- *The new business* has, by its nature, no proved trading record to show to potential investors.
- *Potential investors* are likely to be deterred by dependence on the personal commitment of an individual founder of the business, in case his or her services are withdrawn.

Most of our sample businesses were drawn to the MIDAS competition by the opportunity to boost their own equity with the prize money, and would clearly be reluctant to share the profits of their ingenuity. Where outside investors in the equity have come in to provide finance, some ingenious devices to control the management of the business have been used. Thus one company issued voting shares to the founders, who managed the business, and non-voting shares to other investors. Another company issued two different classes of share, each carrying the right to appoint two directors; each of the two families involved owned one of the classes of share, ensuring that although one family had invested more equity than the other each family had an equal hand in controlling the business.

In one case four entrepreneurs together formed a highly professional team operating in a highly technical industry. Needing an injection of equity well beyond their own resources, they obtained a large investment from a small investment company, in fact being left with only a minority share in the equity to share among themselves. In practice, the four entrepreneurs were able to run the business without interference and eventually to buy out the majority interest on favourable terms when the company proved successful. The source of their strength was that their management skills were vital to the business, and so they were able to get their way with the investment company by threatening to resign as directors if opposed.

Since outside equity investment was considered both unavailable and undesirable by most of our sample, they were left to find the initial equity from their own resources. We will now look at the possible sources available to them.

First, redundancy payments, terminal gratuities and inheritances. The first two, of course, commonly coincide with the recipient being in search of an occupation, and therefore open to the idea of a business venture. We had few such sources of finance in our sample, perhaps because the MIDAS scheme attracts innovators while those with spare money to invest tend to look at established businesses. There is a tendency for those whose motivation is to find a 'home' for their money rather than to implement a long-held idea to produce rather 'half baked' ideas. Thus one applicant proposed a scheme to manufacture a product which he clearly thought to be original, as a way of profitably employing a terminal gratuity. In fact the product concerned was already manufactured by an existing business, and on sale at a price below the applicant's expected cost of production!

A second source of finance is savings. The problem with

reliance on savings is that the higher the existing income of the entrepreneur, the higher the established standard of living and therefore the drawings which must be made from the profits of the business. There is a distinct tendency for entrepreneurs to make wildly optimistic assumptions about the amounts on which they will be able to live while their businesses grow. Thus one applicant, earning £20,000 a year from his current job, planned to draw only £400 per month from the business. His accumulated savings available for investment in the business were not so large as to suggest this could be a realistic target!

Where there is more than one person involved in the business then it is possible for the partners to accumulate savings to launch the business by moral pressure on each other. One group of three partners had agreed to open a business bank account, into which each paid a monthly standing order.

Another way of launching a business is to commence on a spare time basis with earnings from a full-time job covering living expenses and also, perhaps, contributing to business expenses. The practicality of this approach depends on the nature of the current employment. To give three examples:

- a factory worker went on to night shifts, running his business during the day;
- a salesman had totally flexible working hours subject to achieving his targets. He visited his personal customers while visiting his employer's customers in the same area;
- by contrast, three technicians planned to set up a business competing with their existing employer. They knew that as soon as their intention to set up business became known their existing employment would be terminated.

A partner's earnings can provide another source of finance. A variation of the use of current personal earnings is that initially one partner works for the business full time while the other partner(s) continue in permanent employment and support the business financially. Such an arrangement depends heavily on mutual trust! It is a particularly common approach where a husband and wife set up in business, but even there difficulties can arise. For example, in one case a husband in a particularly sensitive job had to obtain special permission from his employer for his wife to set up in business.

The sale of, or a loan raised on the security of, personal property is a popular method of raising money. It was common for applicants to the MIDAS scheme to propose to raise a second mortgage on their own home, or alternatively to offer a second mortgage on their own home to the bank as security for a loan to the business. Such an approach does, of course, involve considerable personal risk. If the business is unsuccessful the entrepreneur faces the prospect of emerging not only jobless and broke, but also homeless into the bargain!

One of the problems faced by an innovative new business is that a large amount of money, and an even more substantial amount of the founder's time, can often be spent on setting up the business, covering items such as product and market research. Conventional accounting practices fail, by and large, to recognize as an asset investment in such 'intangible' benefits. Thus a large part of the entrepreneur's investment is swallowed by expenditure that will not be reflected in the accounts, and therefore will not serve to convince potential lenders that the owners have contributed a fair share of equity to the business. One company had been successful in persuading their auditors that a large amount of expenditure involved in developing a new machine should be recorded as an asset, 'development expenditure', in the accounts, and so contrived to show a very much healthier balance sheet than would otherwise be the case. Accountants have strict rules limiting the circumstances in which such an accounting treatment is permitted, and this business was lucky to have auditors who applied the rules in a rather liberal spirit.

Once a business is launched equity also comes from profits earned and retained by the business. All the businesses we looked at clearly regarded the retention of profits as a major source of finance. Indeed, one business currently employing some ten staff claims to have started with an initial investment of £5 and to have been built up entirely with retained profits.

Seeking Borrowing

Most applicants to MIDAS expected to borrow from a bank in order to launch their businesses. One of the attractions of the MIDAS scheme at that time was that a guarantee to cover up to £50,000 of bank borrowing was available to winners. This part of the package of prizes undoubtedly attracted more interest from applicants than any other, for three reasons:

- the guarantee carried with it a willingness by the bank to offer a somewhat lower interest rate than usual for such propositions;
- the availability of the guarantee substantially increased the chances of obtaining a loan, particularly for those applicants who had little in the way of personal security to offer;
- as an alternative to the normal bank requirement to provide a personal security, the guarantee was attractive to some applicants who were not willing to incur the personal liability of guaranteeing the loan themselves.

In recent years the major banks have tried to respond to the traditional criticism that they did not provide enough support to emerging businesses, and certainly the experiences of MIDAS applicants in seeking bank borrowing tended to reflect this.

Among our sample loan applications were almost invariably supported by cash flow forecasts, showing forecast inflows and outflows of cash on a month-by-month basis. In some cases applicants had prepared these themselves, often on the basis of a small amount of business training. For example, an engineer whose only business training consisted of a year on part-time evening course produced a highly professional forecast. Some applicants had employed professional accountancy firms to prepare forecasts for them. There was a tendency for forecasts to be prepared on the basis of highly optimistic assumptions, particularly assuming prompt payment by customers! Professional accountancy firms normally added a disclaimer pointing out that they were responsible only for the calculations, not for the assumptions. It is, perhaps, indicative of the legalistic training of accountants in the UK that they are more effective at disclaiming responsibility than at persuading their clients to take a commercially realistic view.

While banks tended to be willing to lend on most well-presented propositions, they were anxious to ensure full personal guarantees and security from loan applicants. In several cases, owners of limited companies decided not to expand because they did not want to incur this personal commitment. This anxiety to maximize security led, in the following example, to a bank pressing very poor advice on a client.

A businessman, who operated through a limited company, decided to buy premises in his own name and rent them to the company. The bank tried to persuade him to buy the premises in the name of the company, even though this would have had substantial tax disadvantages. Eventually the bank reluctantly accepted that the building should be owned privately and pledged as security to cover loans to the company, a mechanism that gave the bank full protection while avoiding the tax consequences of direct ownership by the company.

Bank managers seem rather coy about admitting that they are covering their risk by taking security. Almost without exception, they affirm that their objective is to ensure the 'commitment' of the borrower.

The other major source of borrowing for a new business is trade credit offered by suppliers (examples of how this may be exploited were offered in chapter 1). In some cases, however, suppliers insist on a record of trading before allowing credit. One amusing example of this arose for a business which had applied to a local authority to rent special 'starter unit' premises designed for new businesses. Incredibly, they were asked to produce accounts covering their past five years' trading! Most of our sample, however, managed to obtain the supply of goods on credit terms.

Impact of Cash Shortages on Activity

So far we have considered the ways in which the owners of the businesses in our sample went about raising the cash they needed to operate. We will now consider how they adapted the way in which they carried on business in order to cope with cash shortages.

Discovering how to minimize the investment in tangible fixed assets was essential to the success of several of our businesses. For example:

- a nightclub owner wanted to install a new stage and related fittings. By supervising the construction himself, employing hired labour, he managed to cut the cost by over two-thirds compared with the price quoted by contractors;
- to avoid the costs of equipping a small factory Victoria East, considered in detail below, had her product made up by outworkers;
- an inventor devised a production process for a particular product which involved only a fraction of the capital investment required by traditional methods, and therefore made it possible to produce on a small scale.

By contrast, a number of applicants to MIDAS seemed unaware of the opportunities to avoid heavy investment in fixed assets by sub-contracting work out; as a result, their propositions not only involved them in seeking large sums of money to finance expensive plant, but also committed them to launching their product on a large scale to cover overheads.

One point to emerge was that a number of our sample felt an emotional involvement with their premises and production processes that led to an arguably excessive investment in fixed assets. For example, when asked why he wanted to produce his product personally rather than sub-contract the work, an inventor explained that a large part of his motive for launching his business was that it constituted an extension of his 'hobby'. Another business, with the capacity to expand rapidly, chose to buy rather than rent premises, even though this left limited cash available to finance working capital needs.

Investment in intangible expenditure, such as advertising, research, and staff training, tends to be committed with some reluctance, and is often undertaken on a 'do it yourself' basis. In some cases this can be very successful. For example, James Finn of Leather Fashions is an expert photographer and he produced a mail order catalogue at a fraction of the normal cost. However, reliance on self-taught skills developed in a hurry can be dangerously misleading. For example, one MIDAS applicant claimed an unbelievably favourable response to market research relating to a product with apparently limited appeal. On investigation we found that the applicant had performed the market research interviews personally, using a poorly drafted set of questions likely to produce a misleadingly favourable response. In another example one of our sample learned the need for expert advice on marketing very painfully, spending £1,000 on a series of advertisements that produced just £60 of business.

The third factor that tends to absorb the financial resources of a business is the need to provide for increased working capital requirements as trade expands. We have already seen that cash flow forecasts tended to be somewhat optimistic in this respect. A number of MIDAS applicants seemed to assume they could delay payment for extra goods supplied until they received cash from new customers; clearly an unrealistic assumption given the time gap between buying and selling goods. Techniques used to minimize the amount of working capital employed included:

- one business offered a cash discount of 20 per cent to customers paying within 14 days. Such a large discount, clearly very much higher than normal discounts which tend to reflect market rates of interest, was generally taken up. The approach was only practical because the business had a unique high quality product which commanded a high price;
- one importer brought in supplies by air when required,

to avoid having cash tied up during shipping time. This was admitted to be a high cost expedient, forced on the business by necessity.

- one business selling its output through a single retail outlet had too much cash tied up in stock, and held a special one-day sale in a hall hired over a hundred miles away. This enabled the business to clear stock without undercutting its own local trading position.

Comparison of Response

The ways in which a shortage of working capital can affect a new business are highlighted by a comparison of two businesses in our sample – Victoria East and Leather Fashions. Victoria East started in business as a designer and manufacturer of high quality Christmas stockings and has expanded her product range to include gift bags, toy bags and shoe bags. Leather Fashions are a husband and wife team who design and manufacture high fashion, high quality leather garments mainly for women. The two businesses are therefore comparable both in their production process and in the nature of their market.

Victoria East

One of the factors that influenced Victoria East in her choice of business activity was that the product could be produced from reasonably priced materials with ordinary domestic household sewing equipment. Thus no substantial initial outlay was required. She produced an initial collection of samples which she then took to the chief buyer of a major up-market London store. This led to her first orders, and she then procured orders from the other major London stores in the same way.

The profit earned on these first orders, plus resources of her own which she had put into the business initially, were together sufficient to enable her to put together an impressive display for the Earl's Court toy fair. Victoria East sees trade fairs as an essential part of marketing her type of product, and takes the view that it is important to mount a highly professional presentation. Trade fairs are expensive, both in terms of the unavoidable costs of participation and in terms of the cash tied up in a sufficiently wide range of goods for display.

The investment proved worth while, producing orders from a number of retailers and also an approach from a major charity interested in ordering a large supply of Christmas stockings designed to reflect their field of operation. The design produced for the charity delighted them and resulted in a large order.

Following the fair, therefore, Victoria East had three cash problems: how to finance an expansion of her manufacturing capacity; how to finance the working capital tied up in the expanded business; how to finance the stock tied up in the very large order for the charity.

The first problem was solved by a decision to employ outworkers, using their own machinery, to produce the goods. Besides avoiding heavy capital expenditure, this approach also saved the business from the heavy fixed costs of employing staff and incurring factory overheads. The problems of supervising a workplace were avoided, allowing Victoria East to devote her time to selling and design. She was fortunate in being located in a part of the country where there was a strong local tradition of textile outwork, so that highly trained workers were easily found.

The second problem of financing the overall increase in the level of activity was tackled by approaching the bank for an overdraft facility. Victoria East drew on her experience as a personal assistant in large companies to put together a highly professional presentation, including detailed profit and cash flow projections. The loan was granted, and repaid within the agreed period. Since that experience the bank has been most cooperative in providing overdraft facilities when approached.

The third problem related to the financing of working capital for the very large order from the national charity. In this case an approach was made to the customer explaining the tight working capital constraints on this new business and suggesting breaking down the order into three parts, each to be paid for following delivery. The customer appreciated the situation and fell in with the suggestion.

Following the successful launch of the business, Victoria East considered ways in which the product range could be expanded. She produced designs for a range of gift bags, toy bags and shoe bags. One factor in her mind at this stage was the desirability of spreading her trade away from a concentration on Christmas, so as to ease the seasonal cash flow problem. The expanded product range was presented at the Birmingham Gift Fair, again involving a substantial outlay in order to achieve the highest possible quality of presentation. The exhibition at the gift fair was a great success, particularly in opening up export markets such as Japan, the USA, Singapore and Kuwait.

Leather Fashions

Leather Fashions was first launched in the early 1970s, and was then re-launched in the mid-1970s. The history of the first launch illustrates how an emerging business can be stifled at birth through pressures on cash flow, while the history of the development of the business since the re-launch illustrates how the form of a business can be dictated by response to short term cash flow pressures.

James and Delia Finn, the couple who launched Leather Fashions, initially commenced business on a very small scale, selling leather through a shop in their home town on a sale or return basis. They then decided to make a batch of samples and try to break into the London market. At that time they had so little awareness of normal commercial practices they did not appreciate that most large businesses would have a specialist buying office. Eventually they made contact with the buyer at a major London store, who was impressed by their product and even promised to arrange for them to be paid seven days after the supply of goods. At this stage they appeared to be on the verge of a major success. Unhappily they met, at the same time, an agent who promised to market their goods on condition that all their work be marketed through him, including supplies to the London store with which they had already made contact. When they delivered their first consignment, they learned to their horror that the agent had arranged 90 day payment terms. In the ensuing arguments, seeking early payment, the goods were returned to them. Following this distressing experience the Finns decided that self-employment was not for them.

Some two years later they started again on a part-time basis, selling from market stalls. They found this to be successful and devoted themselves full time to the business. After a year they rented a small shop with a workshop, but were still so short of working capital that they were unable to carry adequate stocks. Making a virtue of necessity, they carried a small stock of samples and made goods to measure for customers. Another year passed and they expanded into mail order, attracted by the prospect of receiving cash with each order and the fact that no stock had to be carried; we have already mentioned that James Finn's photography skills applied to production of a catalogue helped to make mail order a success for Leather Fashions.

By 1980 trade had slackened off – because of the recession, the Finns believed – and they sold the lease on their shop. Thereafter they operated from home, supplying a shop owner they knew locally and continuing with their mail order trade. In that year, however, came their big break-through. A photograph in a fashion magazine attracted the attention of the organizers of a trade fair, who invited them to exhibit. Their product created tremendous interest, and they found themselves overwhelmed with orders.

Following their trade fair success, the Finns had to expand their production capacity rapidly. This led to three problems:

1 The obvious problems of an increased working capital requirement, which could only be met in part by bank overdraft finance. For example, they had to turn down a major export order because of shortage of finance;
2 Their landlord raised objections to the expansion of manufacturing activity in a private house, and it became necessary to find commercial premises. The time taken up in fitting out new premises and coping with obstruction from the planning authorities took up much needed

management time, as well as increasing overheads;

3 While the Finns worked on the design and selling side, they reposed excessive confidence in an employee responsible for handling the production side. This employee abused his position of trust by stealing expensive raw materials, causing substantial loss both through the theft and through disruption of production.

Following these setbacks, the Finns have now cut back on the number of trade fairs they attend, seeking to achieve more from each fair they do attend. The business has survived its difficulties, but the major factor holding back further expansion continues to be shortage of capital.

A comparison of Leather Fashions and Victoria East shows how the latter planned her business from the start with an eye on the constraints imposed by a shortage of cash, while at the same time using her business skills to get round difficulties. Examples of her planning are:

- her choice of a product that could be produced without a large initial investment of equipment;
- the avoidance of setting up a manufacturing unit by the use of outworkers;
- expansion of the product range in a way that avoided seasonal cash flow problems.

Examples of her skill at coping with difficulties are:

- the willingness to discuss her cashflow problem frankly with her first large customer, securing more helpful payment terms;
- her business-like relations with the bank, proving her reliability by a professional approach and by a realistic loan proposal which she was able to comply with.

One further point to note, which in large measure can be seen as the source of Victoria East's success, is that having identified the substantial outlay on trade fairs as essential she invested the necessary cash without trying to achieve 'false economies'. The small business owner is often reluctant to incur the substantial expenditure involved in such an intangible investment.

The emergence of Leather Fashions has been constantly hampered by cash flow difficulties, and the survival of the business can be seen as largely attributable to the originality and quality of the product. Both the early unhappy experience of selling through a London agent, and the later experience of being unable to take advantage of a large export order, illustrate the difficulties that arise when large organizations fail to take into account the special cash flow problems that can arise in their dealings with small emerging businesses.

8 The Market Niche

One of the themes of this book has been that the survival of a small business is, at its best, precarious; but by developing control over a specific area of the market in which it operates, a small business may achieve a surprising degree of stability. In such cases the size of the market area may be relatively unimportant; it is rather the ability to become a specialist in that area which can be capitalized upon. Strategies are then developed to maintain, protect and develop this specific area of the market. Gradually, the small business creates a specialized market area or 'market niche' which it alone is equipped to serve.

In this chapter we shall highlight the idea of the market niche as it relates to small business. We make two contentions. First, a 'nicher's' skill is to develop a specialism. This can be either in terms of the product, for example unique design as exemplified by Victoria East, or as a specialism in terms of customer, for example, serving primarily retailers, as instanced by Polstar (see chapter 4) and European Energy Resources (see chapter 2). The second contention is that ideally strategies are developed by the small business to protect its niche. These strategies are heterogenous, each set of strategies reflecting the characteristics and peculiarities of the market for which they were developed.

The Niche in Relation to the Rest of the Market?

In simple terms the market may be depicted as a complex array of different sized organizations each trying to secure a share of the market. Within each industry there tends to be domination by a few large organizations or companies. In order to compete with each other on this grander scale these large companies may be forced to ignore or overlook certain operations. These operations may, for example, entail using highly skilled labour, to produce a customized or high quality product, or perhaps a specific operation demands a unique piece of machinery, but only a specialized part of the market wants the item so machined. In each case a large company may feel that this operation does not fit in with the rest of its production. So a large firm with a problem of this nature might welcome a small business specializing in that particular area. These ignored or discarded operations are likely to be specialized and will not be a major part of a market as big business would hardly allow a viable area to slip through its fingers. Hence these discarded operations may not involve any clash with big business. Small businesses will be attracted to such areas. They will suit small businesses in the sense that, as small businesses need to command and oversee an area, the area should not be too complex.

In short, a market niche has the qualities of being specialized in some way, of affording the small firm something of 'a cockpit view' of its area of operation, while most likely avoiding competition with big companies. Several of the small businesses in our case study display some or all of these features.

The Discovery of a Niche

This myth of 'discovery' must first be corrected. The idea of an entrepreneur waking up one morning with a brilliant idea as to which part of the market he or she can conquer today, is very attractive. Unfortunately reality demands considerably more than a bright idea to create a market. The word 'create' is the key to the problem, niches are seldom discovered ready-made, they need to be developed or created.

So what is it that leads to the creation of a niche? As was suggested in chapter 2 when the sample of businesses was introduced, one of the major factors is that of the entrepreneur's education, where 'education' is taken in its widest sense, including previous employment. A past job in a similar area allows background knowledge to be gained. Insight into the area can lead to possible ideas for developing a small business through knowing that an area is either badly covered or by seeing a 'hole' in the market which would lend itself to niche creation. This knowledge linked with networks of contacts built up over a number of years will help pave the way for a new business venture. These factors help lower the risk level and act almost as a metaphorical 'toe in the water' before plunging into the world of small business.

Case Studies

Most of our chosen small businesses tell the story of entrepreneurs who have successfully created and developed a niche. Each company has its own style of operation which is a mix between the market in which it works and the personality of the entrepreneur. Likewise, their strategies devised for niche protection are again influenced by market area and entrepreneurial personality . Each company can be taken individually to show different approaches and strategies for niche protection.

European Energy Resources

The market niche developed by this particular company is that of acting as an intermediary between large manufacturers and a variety of end-users. The company buys batteries in bulk from large manufacturers, assembles them in all sorts of shapes, sizes and combinations to suit the needs of a wide variety of customers. The arrangement works well because large manufacturing companies do not want the bother of assembly for complicated orders, often for relatively small customers. Small customers in their turn usually cannot afford, nor have space, for buying in bulk. Thus there is a gap between the manufacturers' wants and the needs of customers. The operations of European Energy Resources

(EER) show how such a gap can be successfully bridged in terms of a niche for a third party. It is significant that manufacturers now automatically contract out their smaller orders to EER. It is also interesting that the company has a very promising turnover considering its short life to date.

Strategies For Now?

For the small business, strategies for breaking into a market must also take into account the very real problem of keeping costs to a minimum. The ability to break into a market by working within recognized boundaries and keeping costs low is a skillful operation.

As has been underlined at several points throughout this book, the management of limited capital resources is a tricky matter when building up a small business. The first strategy successfully adopted by EER is one of a minimum outlay resulting in orders that produce a profit available for re-investment into the company. Buying batteries in bulk, assembling, re-packaging or factoring them is a low cost business: neither high cost machinery nor skilled labour is required. Other overheads such as rent were kept right down at the start with the business established and continued for some time with just two people working in and from one room over a shop. Contact with customers was in the form of telephone conversations. This helped keep costs down by making plush office furnishings unnecessary. Using the telephone when dealing with customers has other spin-offs, which takes us on to the second strategy employed by the company, that of image development as a strategy for success.

By image development we do not mean simply a corporate image, but in more general terms the way in which the firm is perceived by others. In the case of this business, other companies were not actively discouraged from thinking that the firm was larger than its actual size. This strategy fits in with the entrepreneur's knowledge of the market area and his past experience working as a promotions manager for a patents company. In each case he was made aware that confidence and therefore orders were placed with safe and efficient companies and that these credentials were usually attributed to bigger companies.

Conveying this image of a safe, efficient (and larger) company was managed in several ways. In the early days telephone dealings neutralized the humble nature of the office premises. The telephone was again used to advantage by the company, in that when customers contacted the company they talked with someone who not only knew the product area, but was fluent in big business parlance. The company substantiated these favourable first impressions by investing in a comprehensive paperwork system with invoicing slips, compliment slips, credit notes, and so on, thereby ensuring that EER's paperwork system fitted in with that of larger companies. Another stroke of genius, as well as practicality, was dispatching orders to customers by Securicor – again promoting the image of a large and efficient firm.

Victoria East

Victoria East's company was described in chapter 7, where her use of outworkers was given as a good example of the reduction of capital outlay by a small firm. Her company designs and manufactures high quality Christmas stockings. The market niche aimed at is that of the top-of-the-market shops and customers. The stocking design is bright and effective, the stockings are made up in felt and a large variety of hand stitched motifs allows many variations in final product. The stockings, although primarily designed for children, also appeal to adult tastes. Of late the business has diversified and also manufactures gift, toy and shoe bags.

The previous discussion of EER showed us a market strategy in which, among other things, a small company produced an expansive corporate image. By contrast, Victoria East emphasizes the one-woman nature of her business, using her charismatic personality to sell both the company and its products. Her strategy is one which flouts rather than conforms to market conventions. This strategy links strong design flair with an understanding and confidence in dealing with people. Her previous job experience, as a personal assistant to several directors of large firms, although not directly related to her small business venture, provided her with vicarious business experience and an understanding of the workings of senior management.

Victoria East realized there were no high quality Christmas stockings on the market and decided to aim at this Christmas market first. It has the advantage that both stores and customers are in a buying frame of mind, although the drawback is that it is a very seasonal market.

Personality is the key to Victoria East's démarche, an excellent example of this in action being her initial steps in opening up the market. She had a clear idea of the customer type she was hoping to attract – they would shop in top London department stores. It therefore seemed obvious that the first people to contact would be the buyers in these stores. Using this direct approach Victoria East broke all the conventions. She simply made up some samples and walked into a top department store with a request to see the chief buyer. This personal approach allowed her to bypass a number of 'problem areas' such as brochure design, corporate image etc., all of which take time and money. Sending written material also allows the store time to think about reasons why it should not be interested in the product. Using a direct approach, she received positive encouragement and orders were placed. The London market was captured at a stroke. The brightly coloured festive look of the stockings was perfect for seasonal window displays and they were used widely, thus ensuring immediate 24-hour publicity.

Moving On

The coup with the London department stores had demonstrated that this company could produce reasonable quantities of high quality Christmas stockings. An extension of the market was needed, since relying upon old customers for a steady trade may be dangerous, allowing complacency and not ensuring the challenge which is needed to keep a company growing. The potential market was huge but vague, and rather than attempting to contact organizations individually, Victoria East decided to put her favoured phrase 'take the gamble and go' into practice and have a stall at a trade fair.

The major advantage of trade fairs is that they bring the potentially interested customers to the company. This is vital for a small company where trying to seek these people out might involve huge amounts of both time and energy. The major disadvantage of entering a trade fair is one of up-front cost, although in reality it may only cost as much as an advertisement in a nationwide magazine and secure interest and orders well above the return from such an advertisement.

To maximize the gains from a trade fair it helps to understand the principles upon which they work. In a trade fair potential customers are viewing hundreds of stalls and meeting proprietors on each. Presentation is everything, it must attract interest in the first place, but also create an enduring impression. For Victoria East stall design and presentation was a natural strength and as a result the trade fair paid off handsomely.

The company's ability to mass produce stockings, giving them a degree of originality simply by changing the motif, made the stockings particularly attractive to charities with Christmas mail order schemes. At her first fair the RSPB, NSPCC and the Wildfowl Trust all placed such orders. These were big orders, but such charities do tend to concentrate upon a particular line for only one year.

A second trade fair was attended deliberately to extend the market. This was a toy fair, and Victoria East concentrated upon the idea of toy bags rather than stockings. These were again made up in brightly coloured felt with a motif. The expansion in markets this time took the company world wide, with interest expressed by Japan, Singapore and the United States. One line requested by a customer was a toy bag with a camel motif which is is now being exported to Kuwait. This success in turn presented a challenge to production.

Small businesses do not have complex organizational structures. Decisions about production can be taken in terms of what best suits the entrepreneur. The production of stockings and bags works like a production line, with each worker having a particular skill. The motifs, for example, are hand stitched, whereas the bag or stocking is machine stitched. However, a factory creates many headaches in terms of cost of the rented space, machinery and administration. Taking these factors into account, and linking these with personal factors such as wanting to work at home in order to be with her daughter, Victoria East decided to manufacture her products using outworkers.

The company is located in Derbyshire, which has a tradition of textile production. By utilizing local outworkers who were used to high quality production but who had been made recently redundant due to the collapse of another textile manufacturer, Victoria East gained a workforce who knew what was expected and were eager for the work. Initially she had to transport the partly completed stockings and bags between the women in order for the next stage to be completed. The women developed social links, however, and they now organize the exchange of the pieces, with Victoria East picking up a finished batch of stockings or bags at the end of each week. What has developed is a family feeling – one way in which standards are kept so high. Another factor is pride in the work, carried to the smallest detail (only Victoria East herself is allowed to draw the faces on the snowmen!).

We have seen in several of the companies discussed in this book how the flexibility of the small business helps ensure the high quality often required to exploit a market. Victoria East's belief in small firms leads her to use other small businesses as much as possible. Her printer, for example, is a local man who produces name cards, product wrapping and so on. As with the goods themselves a high standard of presentation is vital. The strategy of developing a small business community is also useful. Other small businesses have a similar standard of pride and interest in the finished product. They enjoy a challenge and out of both interest and economic necessity are prepared to say 'yes' more often than a bigger business might. Versatility is a strength of the smaller business, and this can allow a product a greater degree of individuality.

The niche that Victoria East occupies is one which avoids

competing with mass producers in Taiwan. It is protected from competition by the virtuosity of design. Maintenance of quality and the flexibility of production allow her to develop new ideas and products, so that although markets may change, the chances are that the company will keep pace.

Light Fantastic

Light Fantastic is a small business concerned with making holograms (three-dimensional images composed of light). Although their existence has been long understood in theoretical physics, it is only very lately, and almost completely due to the efforts of this company, that holography has been recognized as both an advertising tool and an art medium.

What makes Light Fantastic of interest in the context of our discussion of the market niche is that so far we have seen niches developed from existing areas, whereas Light Fantastic did not have to find an area in which it could move freely without treading on other people's toes. On the contrary, it had a completely open market. Due to the usual constraints faced by small business, however, those of size and finance, it still had to create a niche which it could shape to its own strengths.

The niche the company has developed is that of making holograms both for private customers and for companies to use in advertising. This is a fairly central position in the market and puts the firm at the forefront of holographic development in Britain.

Removing as many risks as possible in an innovative enterprise is bound to enhance the chances of success. One way of limiting risks is by putting up both a technical and managerial understanding of the area of operations. Peter Woodd, the managing director of the company, explained to us that he had taken this into account when he set up Light Fantastic in 1982. He had previously worked in Holoco, part of a business empire built by the rock group 'The Who', where he had had both the money and the freedom to experiment with the medium and discover its potential.

Creating an Image

As with all innovations, Peter Woodd knew that the first generation of products would be expensive, largely due to lack of competition and the prices demanded by holographic artists for their 'one-off' pieces. Such considerations demanded a high class profile and a manner of awakening the market which was in itself bright and interesting. Full page advertisements, however spectacular, could not really convey the message of holography. It was realized that holography needs to be seen to be sold. The answer, it seemed, was to open Britain's first retail holographic gallery. The company moved into available premises (at reasonable rates) in the (now exclusive) Covent Garden Centre. Peter Woodd planned the gallery's interior himself. The environment he created, with an open plan gallery and unobtrusive electronic music, provided the right setting for so new a medium.

'Lazy' Marketing

The gallery contains many different holograms, from an image of a Perrier water bottle, through to abstract designs. Each piece has a purpose, appealing to different customers. The Perrier bottle is a clear example of holography as an advertising tool, while other images show either the fun side of holography or its newest technical advances. This is an almost 'lazy' way of marketing, of allowing customers to look at the product in a carefully designed environment and then to reflect upon this at their leisure.

Using the gallery as a strategy, Light Fantastic alerted the market to the new medium. The holograms shown suggested the various ways in which holography could be used. By suggesting these possible developments, Light Fantastic was introducing itself as a company that could make holographic dreams come true. The company having taken the pro-active step of showing holography to the market, it was now up to the customers to react, and from these reactions Light Fantastic could plan its next development.

Commercial customers, like ordinary visitors, tend to come

to the gallery personally, having heard about it by word of mouth. Perhaps surprisingly, Light Fantastic have found advertising agencies have had no part in directing customers towards using holography. Apparently it is hard to break away from two-dimensional thinking. The lazy marketing principle of allowing people time to reflect upon their visit works as well for commercial customers as for individual buyers. If a commercial customer asks to talk to someone in the company it will mean that he is already convinced of the use of holography, and the job of the company becomes one of merely outlining the full potential of the product and meeting the customer's demands.

With such a potential customer expressing an interest the company can come into its own. Light Fantastic has a strong team. The first person that the interested party will meet is the marketing director, George McCoullough. The 'office' overlooks the gallery and it is here, at the hub of things, that the marketing director is to be found. This has advantages for both the customer and the company. The customer can make immediate contact with someone who readily converts their needs into a viable plan. The company is able to turn the enthusiasm expressed by the customer to its advantage, and appears efficient and interested. All in all, a feeling of goodwill is generated. As a response to this close contact, Light Fantastic has found it necessary to minimize its 'high tech' nature, as this can tend to frighten many people. They attempt to 'de-mystify' holography for their commercial customers by involving them as much as possible in the project. Listening to the customer and discussing ideas and problems is sound marketing sense. It wins the customer's confidence and promotes a feeling of loyalty.

Company Expansion

Having successfully awoken the market to holography and picked a key area as its niche, the reaction of customers in terms of inquiries and projects undertaken led to the decision to expand by setting up a production unit. Formerly the production of the holograms had been contracted out. The necessary extension of control over the whole process reflects the characteristics of this dynamic market. As a strategy it ensures that the company is in the forefront of technological advance.

The independence that Light Fantastic has gained from the production function allows a corresponding increase in its responsiveness to customer demands. This can be seen working at its best in the complete advertising package offered to the customer where the company maximizes its ability to fuse both imaginative marketing ideas with practical possibilities.

In summary, we might say that Light Fantastic has used several different strategies both to develop and maintain its niche. By almost playing down the medium and making it 'user-friendly', it has attracted an interest from business which is usually conservative about such developments. Towards its private customers it has also applied a similar strategy. By 'listening to the customer' in a very literal sense, the company was able to commission certain styles of holograms. This allowed them to reduce the price and increase sales. An examination of the visitors' book at the Covent Garden gallery showed that customers came from 66 different countries, enough to gain both an award and favourable publicity from the British Tourist Board. These are both clear examples of how easily available information can be used productively. Finally, listening to what the market demanded and acting upon it can also be seen in the development of the company research and development function.

First Find Your Niche...

The trouble with setting out an idea and then illustrating it with reference to good practice is that people may think the process discussed is easy or has to happen that way. So, we will offer a counter example.

The company we will look at is by no means a certain loser (and it is not one of the core sample given in chapter 2), but it has faced a market problem. It has been a winner of two design awards, suggesting that experts felt it was likely to become a successful venture.

The company produces personal trolleys, along the lines of pull-along shopping trolleys. Initially the idea was to produce a trolley which could carry all the extra bits and pieces involved with either picnics or eating out of doors, for example on a camping or caravanning holiday. In the beginning a trolley was exhibited at a leisure fair where it gained favourable comment. The idea of a trolley is not original, but aiming the product at a particular market might have created a niche to be developed and maintained.

Problems in Niche Building

Paradoxically, the wholeness of vision with which the development of a market niche is associated, can lead to a single-mindedness culminating in very narrow vision. This can take two forms. The first manifests itself as a commitment to the product and a striving for perfection through constant readjustment or embellishment of constituent parts. This may backfire because each development leads to new, improved products or variations on a theme. This leads to the second problem, which is that no one area can be a target area, because there are too many variables. This may be inverted to become a 'product blindness' where the inventor of the product can see universal applications for it. Then a regressive spiral develops; as the product is further developed, time and money are invested, but without any market research to discover whether it is what a customer might want. Meanwhile the product is not being sold as the product range is not complete, and as the product range grows so do *potential* markets, meaning that marketing effort and the cash resources to support it are spread ever more thinly. It may be that our trolley company fell into this trap.

First faced with seemingly endless possible markets and therefore without a clear market to aim for, the company decided to place a half-page mail order advertisement in a nationwide magazine. The cost of this was high. If we think back to our other case studies, all the businesses studied in this chapter avoided advertising in this way. Blanket advertising exposes a weakness of the small business, namely that one advertisement is not enough and reminders in the shape of subsequent advertisements are required. Small businesses usually have very limited resources and they cannot afford to follow up, whereas the big company can keep on spending until it starts to win. Not angling the advertisement at any particular group means that it will not immediately appeal to any group. Added to this, mail order advertisements have a notoriously slow response rate.

The firm's next move was to take just one of the products from the product range, in this case a trolley for anglers with its own fold-away seat, and again advertise through a nationwide magazine for anglers. Although this was a specialist magazine the orders were very slow in coming. Subsequent research suggested this was due mainly to an old and established habit of sitting on tackle boxes, the use of a trolley seat involving a loss of credibility among fellow anglers. Further attempts to open this specialist market were frustrated because fishing tackle shops nationwide are independently owned and therefore trying to visit any number of them is logistically difficult for a small business entrepreneur.

In part this sort of difficulty is one of finding a distribution set up. For example, if a chain of stores could be interested in the product, the problem of interesting individual shops would disappear. Although this approach seems promising, it may be that the cost of this particular trolley stops it from being an 'impulse buy'. People would probably buy the trolley at its present price on personal recommendation, but this manner of infiltration is slow and the return for the company not fast enough. On the other hand, lowering the price of the trolley to make it a possible 'impulse buy' would reduce profit margins too drastically to make this a feasible option.

In other words, an estimable company with a good product has a real marketing problem. Several niches are identifiable, yet none seems attainable, with the distributional logistics stacked against the entrepreneur.

Conclusions

We have tried to show that many markets have unoccupied niches. These are unoccupied because of neglect or the inability of existing businesses to fill them. Compared with the rest of the market area, these niches may be small and involve a higher degree of specialization They tend not to trespass upon other people's business areas and therefore do not pose a threat. This lack of competition due to high specialization makes the niches attractive to small businesses.

For exploitation of a niche to become successful it must be big enough to ensure that the company will make a living and have growth potential that allows either expansion within the area, or diversification from it. This point has to be recognized by the small business itself, where the strategy for survival is flexibility and development.

Once the niche has been found or created by the small business, strategies for niche protection need to be developed. The first form of preservation is that of altering and adapting the company so that it matches more exactly the needs of the niche, thus allowing little chance for competition. This niche preservation, and flexibility in developing the niche, are closely related to a good overall understanding of the market.

A small business can also exploit its smallness and presumptive flexibility as a preservation strategy. Small businesses should have the ability to turn round quickly and provide customers with what they want. This, plus a friendly personal touch, may well be enough to secure customer loyalty.

The market niche then appears to be alive and well, and we can see small (and new) businesses exploiting it well into the 1980s. As new ideas are developed there are spin-offs in terms of the niches that can be created. The market is not an exclusively competitive arena ruled by the survival of the fittest; some markets permit, indeed facilitaate, a quite high degree of 'peaceful coexistence'. The trick is to find them.

9 Forms of Originality

At the outset we argued that small businesses are qualitatively different from larger corporations, and inhabit a more immediate and precarious world. This theme has been elaborated, in both the general and the particular by showing, on the one hand the problems and challenges faced by small businesses, and on the other, the strivings and strategems with which small firms respond. These accounts have contained, but not necessarily highlighted, constant allusion to the most potent resource of the small businessman – originality. In this concluding chapter we offer not a summary but an extension of this simple idea, that every small business start-up is an act of originality.

At its simplest the idea is this: those who start businesses and make them work have thought of something other people have not. That something is both variable and composite, and sometimes it has a holistic quality as well. Earlier chapters have offered many examples of this variety – the entrepreneur has a design for a new or improved product, or an understanding of how to make something better, an idea for a new service that people will pay for, a vision of a new application, of an unexploited market, of a demand unsatisfied. Let us take up instead the idea that this originality may be composite.

We will start with a straightforward example, Marlec Engineering and their wind-powered generators. This is not simply a case of a brilliant practical engineer who can develop a product that breaks through earlier limitations. No, here is an entrepreneur with previous business experience, whose engineering abilities are conjoined with appreciation of user needs, trade knowledge and the know-how to exploit sales outlets. Note that this entrepreneur does not have sales experience, does not think of himself as a salesman and does not employ any salesmen, but he still sells a lot.

Or consider Victoria East and the Christmas stockings and toy bags. What is original about her performance? Obviously, it is her flair for design, but again there are other dimensions. It is design flair plus awareness of having promotional drive, plus an inspired organization of production that bypasses all the usual problems, plus seeing a gap at the top end of the market. The originality is in seeing that all these factors together can produce a viable, indeed ebullient, business.

The case of Pro Stock Glass takes the argument further. Pro Stock are supplying glass fibre bolt-on panels and extras to the racing car, stock car and general motor enthusiast market. From table 2.7 (p.28) it is clear at a glance that the partners have an enviable array of relevant skills: they know how to make and drive cars, how to paint them, service them, repair them and probably sell them. They also know what to do with glass fibre, how to make the moulds, work with it and deliver the goods. But there is more to it than that. They have, to use the vague and convenient phrase, 'trade knowledge'. Let us look at it more closely.

The world of the motor (racing) enthusiast is geographically dispersed, but it is a community of interest, quite a compact one, where a lot of people know each other and attend the same events. Anyone who frequents these knows not only the personalities but the dealers and suppliers and the things they trade in. It is also a world that has its own style, and in the expression of this style there are things enthusiasts will buy, in both senses, and things they won't. You have to know this world to be able to design bolt-on panels because there is not a finite list of body accessories written down anywhere, or codified specifications on their curves and contours. It is all about style and what goes and what the peer group will be impressed by. Not everybody who belongs to this world of motor enthusiasts becomes a supplier to it, however, and an innovative supplier at that. The Pro Stock partners know something else, quite practical. They know who the other suppliers of these accessories are – and they are principally American and relatively expensive.

In other words, trade knowledge may cover a range of things from the intangible understanding of what people will like, through the practicalities of suppliers and retail outlets and knowledge of relevant magazines and advertising, to where to make contacts and what the competitors are charging. The originality of the Pro Stock partners is to bring all that together. This is the point at which the composite becomes the holistic.

Inhalation Therapy Products, which produces hospital consumables, is a good illustration of originality in the form of understanding a whole market and its operation. The entrepreneur here has looked at this market world wide and appreciated that the USA is bound to be the leader in terms of product innovation and the R & D that goes with it. It is not just that America is large and rich; the critical thing is that it has a *private* medical system, so there will be competition and demand for ever-more refined and presumptively effective drugs and treatment aids. So the USA is bound to lead, and bound to predominate in supplying its own market.

When it comes to supplying Britain, however, the USA is handicapped first by transport costs and at times by a strong dollar. An entrant to this market in Britain does not need to carry an R & D burden or even to be in front. It is well understood that all the breakthroughs will be over there, but there is no reason why enterprising concerns elsewhere should not do a little development work on the second generation of these products and sell successfully in their domestic market.

Another of our companies showing this same kind of originality – the ability to put together a composite operation and locate it effectively in a larger environment – is Ensign Computers. The proprietor in this case sees himself first and foremost as a salesman. His emphasis is probably right and yet this simple label does him less than justice. One might think that a quarter of a century after main frame computers came on to the market there would not be any new applications, that nothing would be left to computerize: but Ensign found something. They appreciated that there are lots of businesses that do contract work for their clients, and these jobs are all somewhat different and on a one-off basis. Hence they have an ever-present need for costing and estimating for potential clients. This costing is a time-consuming and recurrent chore. Ensign therefore developed some estimating systems software.

The first buyers of the estimating system were printing companies; then Ensign started to sell the system to ducting systems (central heating) companies, and found an extensive potential market here in which they could specialize.

It will be clear already that these customers are not for the most part big concerns, and many of them, of course, will have no computer to start with. Ensign have solved this by providing the computer as well. In fact, Ensign acquire relatively small computers from three different larger companies and then rent, lease or hire purchase sell them to Ensign clients along with the appropriately customized estimating systems software. This arrangement not only provides the customer with everything, a one-stop deal, but it means there is some money to be made out of the provision of the computers as well, even if the software is the fulcrum of the operation.

There are other angles. Anyone who supplies hardware can offer customers a maintenance contract, and money can be made out of this even if the maintenance cover is sub-contracted. It is also both possible and desirable to offer customers updates on the software; that is, to offer them the automatic provision of later improvements and refinements to the software package (and the client pays for such updates a sum usually agreed in advance). Ensign has such an update arrangement with its clients which gives Ensign a small additional, but more or less captive, market.

This is an ingenious and composite operation. Sales may be the driving force of this business as an on-going affair, but it is not in any simple sense 'all about sales'.

Originality is also, on occasion, manifest in the quality of a particular kind of decision-making in which small firm proprietors are involved, and this is quite simply, what to spend their money on. There are two basic problems about this, especially for the small new firm. The first is that they do not usually have enough money. The second is that there are some observable tendencies among small businessmen to spend on some things rather than others but these are not always in their best interest. It was suggested earlier, in the discussion of start-up finance (chapter 7), that entrepreneurs like bricks and mortar; they like to build and above all own premises. It makes thems feel good; it is part of being a man of substance. But bricks and mortar are not necessarily the most effective way to deploy scarce resources in a critical period.

Against the background of this argument, it is interesting to note various instances of more imaginative spending among our sample. Polstar was quick to lay out small sums on a business trip to Scandinavia and on the early production of a brochure, and Ensign similarly spent generously on the provision of a one-page advertisement to be used very extensively in a mailing operation to potential customers. Again, at a more substantial level, Victoria East laid out money on trade fairs and Light Fantastic rented premises for their holographic gallery at one of the best sites in London. On the other hand, few of our sample are big spenders on plant and equipment. The predilections of Polstar in distrusting new equipment (1947 was a golden age for equipment) might stand as a symbol for many small firms. Looking to the future only Pro Stock Glass at the time of our last visit was contemplating substantial expenditure on equipment, quite simply to increase productive capacity given what seemed to be a sustained rise in demand.

Entrepreneurs also differ in their ability to structure businesses and devise methods of sheltering profits, the two considerations often being closely linked. Again there is a pattern which can be described with reference to small firms in general rather than our sample in particular. The tendency is for entrepreneurs to rush to form limited companies rather than to operate as partnerships or sole traders. The reasons are clear; it is primarily a matter of security, in that the consequences of business failure are much less awful for the limited company. Also, as with the bricks and mortar enthusiasm referred to earlier, there is a status consideration in the sense that it sounds rather good to be the proprietor of a limited company. On the other hand, this may not always be the best deal, especially in tax terms. Operating as a partnership delays somewhat the actual assessment and payment of tax; furthermore, the partnership form facilitates the carrying forward of losses and offsetting them against later profits, something that may be important in the start-up period. We have, indeed, encountered businesses organized in terms of two legally distinct entities, one registered as a partnership and the other as a limited company, thereby deriving some of the benefits of both statuses.

This dividing a business operation into more that one legal entity can often present advantages in terms of transfers and exchanges between them. Where products are being exported, for example, there may be some gain in creating a separate company to do the exporting. In this case, the manufacturer can sell the product to the exporting entity, thereby becoming liable for VAT, but this tax does not have to be paid instantly but within something like three months. The exporter, however, can reclaim VAT straight away, and it is the time disparity that creates the advantage. Played properly, this can provide working capital as an interest-free government loan!

This structuring and sheltering facility is not, of course, only a matter of the originality of individual entrepreneurs, but also a reflection of the advice they receive. There are now so many agencies for the counselling of small businesses, and indeed the whole small business movement is so much in favour, that the layman may doubt if anything more is needed. We think it may be, and so do some of the entrepreneurs we have interviewed.

The common thread of these observations is to say that sometimes the need for more pro-active advice is expressed. To exaggerate a little, people have said sometimes that they would like a counsellor who would know in advance the sort of problems the entrepreneur was likely to meet and be able to suggest remedies quickly. They wanted someone who would reach across the desk and hang problems and solutions on counsellees while they were still enthusing about the joys of entrepreneurship.

Another thing that sometimes impedes this most desirable state of affairs between counsellor and entrepreneur is that the advisers themselves may practise a too severe division of labour, and we will end with an example of this in action.

The case concerned a small firms adviser who told us of a rather unusual would-be entrepreneur who wanted to set up a fruit farm in Kent and a time-share holiday villa development in Spain at the same time. We asked eagerly if this applicant had been warned of the complications of attempting simultaneously two such disparate and geographically separate operations. 'I didn't do that,' came the reply. 'My job is to tell him how to do his cash flow forecasts.' So perhaps originality has another dimension: that of being able to assess advice.

Bibliography

Articles

Abdelsamad M. H., 'Why small businesses fail', *SAM Advanced Management Journal*, vol. 43, no. 2, 1978.

Abdelsamad M. H., De Genaro G. J. and Wood D. R. jun., 'Fourteen financial pitfalls for small businesses', *SAM Advanced Management Journal*, vol. 42, no. 2, 1977.

Abdelsamad M. H. and Wood D. R., 'Profit planning for small business', *Management World*, vol. 9, no. 3, 1980.

Anderson T., 'OTC route to city finance', *Your Business*, vol. 2, no. 12, 1984.

Anderson T., 'Venture capital', *Your Business*, vol. 2, no. 13, 1984.

Bannock G., 'The clearing banks and small firms', *Lloyds Bank Review*, no. 42, 1981.

Beadley K. and Gelb A., 'Replication and sustainability of the Mondragon Experiment', *British Journal of Industrial Relations*, vol. 20, no. 1, 1982.

Bechhoffer F. and Elliott B., 'The voice of small business and the politics of survival', *Sociology Review*, vol. 26, Feb., 1978.

Belbin R. M., 'Launching new enterprises: some fresh initiatives for tackling unemployment', *Employment Gazette*, vol. 83, 1980.

Bennett D. C., 'State aids to small firms in the European Community', *International Small Business Journal*, vol. 2, no. 1, 1983.

Biggs, S. C., 'Survival of the smallest', *Price Waterhouses Review*, summer/autumn, 1971.

Bollard A., 'Technology, economic change and small firms', *Lloyds Bank Review*, no. 147, 1983.

Bolton Report, 'Report of the committee of inquiry on small firms', HMSO, London, 1971, Cmnd 4811.

Brown R., 'Why small business matters', *Management Today*, Dec., 1976.

Buetow C. P., 'Management and the small corporation', *CA Magazine* vol. 7, no. 4, 1979.

Cannon T., 'Current policies in small firm top management export training and development in the USA', Report to the Nuffield Foundation, 1980.

Cannon T. and Dawson G., 'Developing and export potential of small firms: the role of training', *Industrial and Commercial Training*, July, 1977.

Carroll B., 'Six key ratios for business finance', *Rydges*, vol. 47, no. 6, 1974.

Collis R., 'Ireland puts its money into small business', *International Management*, vol. 37, May, 1982.

Cooley P. L. and Pullen R. J., 'Small business management practices', *American Journal of Small Business*, vol. 4, no. 2, 1979.

Dashwood A., 'Control of state aids in the EEC: prevention and cure under article 93', *Common Market Law Review*, vol. 12, pp. 43–58, 1976.

De Thomas A. R., 'Forecasting the cash budget in the small firm', *American Journal of Small Business*, vol. 4, no. 4, 1980.

Dearden J., 'Profit planning accounting for small firms', *Harvard Business Review*, vol. 41, no. 2, 1963.

Duns Review, 'How small firms raise capital', vol. 113, no. 3, 1979.

Edminster, R. O., 'An empirical test of financial ratio analysis for small business failure prediction', *Journal of Financial and Quantitative Analysis*, March, 1972.

Ekhaugen K., Gronmo S. and Kirby D. A., 'State support to small stores: a Nordic form of consumer policy', *Journal of Consumer Policy*, vol. 4, no. 8, 1980.

Forbes A. M., 'Long range planning for the smaller firm', *Long Range Planning*, vol. 7, no. 2, 1974.

Freeman C., 'The role of small firms in innovation in the UK since 1945', Committee of Inquiry on Small Firms, Research Report no. 6, HMSO, London, 1971.

Friedlander F. and Pickle H., 'Components of effectiveness in small organisations', *Administrative Science Quarterly*, vol. 13, pp. 289–304, 1968.

Ganguly A. and Povey D. A., 'Small firms survey: the international scene', *British Business*, Nov., 1982.

Gasman L., 'Small business and franchising in the USA', *Business Graduate*, vol. 10, spring, 1980.

Gibb A. A. and Ritchie J. E., 'Understanding the process of starting small businesses', *European Small Business Journal*, vol. 1, no. 1, Sept. 1982.

Gilmartin P., 'Survey of sources of finance for small firms', *Business Graduate*, vol. 8, no. 2, 1978.

Hankinson A., 'Small firms' investment and government policy', *International Accountant*, vol. 48, no. 1, 1978.

Hartigan P., 'Why companies fail', *Certified Accountant*, vol. 68, part 6, 1976.

Hosein R., 'How to avoid financial disaster', *Canadian Business*, vol. 48, no. 5, 1975.

Hough J., 'Franchising: an avenue for entry into small business', In, Stanworth J., Westrip A., Watkins D. and Lewis J. eds, *Bolton Ten Years On* (Proceedings of the 1981 Small Business Research Conference) Gower, London, 1982.

Johnson P., 'Policies towards small firms: time for caution?' *Lloyds Bank Review*, no. 129, 1978.

Kirby D. A. and Law D. C., 'The birth and death of small retail units in Britain', *Retail and Distribution Management*, vol. 9, no. 1, 1981.

Kudla R. J., 'Capital rationing in small business', *Journal of Small Business Management*, vol. 18, no. 4, 1980.

Larson C. M. and Clute R. C., 'The failure syndrome', *American Journal of Small Business*, vol. 4, no. 2, 1979.

Lauzen L. G., 'Franchising: another strategy to start your own business', *Management Today (USA)*, vol. 66, no. 1, 1984.

Lever H., 'Small business', *Professional Administration*, vol. 9, no. 5, 1979.

Leyshon A., 'The UK Government small business model: a review', *European Small Business Journal*, vol. 1, Sept., 1982.

London Enterprises Agency, 'Sources of finance for small firms', 1981.

McHugh J., 'The self-employed and the small independent entrepreneur', In, King R. and Nugent N. ed., *Respectable Rebels, Middle Class Campaigns in the 1970s*, London, Hodder & Stoughton, 1979.

McKinlay R. A., 'Some reasons for business failures in Canada', *Cost and Management*, vol. 53, no. 3, 1979.

MacMillan I. C., 'Strategy and flexibility in smaller business', *Long Range Planning*, vol. 8, no. 3, 1975.

Mayo H. B. and Rosenbloom R. 'Ratio analysis for the small business', *Journal of Small Business Management*, vol. 13, no. 1, 1975.

Mitchell J. E., 'Small firms: a critique', *Three Banks Review*, no. 126, 1980.

Mueller A., 'The small firm sector and government support', *Business Graduate*, vol. 8, no. 2, 1978.

Murphy B., 'Financial control in the small firm', *Certified Accountant*, vol. 70, no. 6, 1978.

Parr R., 'The small firm – finance for profit', *Trade and Industry*, Nov., 1979.

Parritt K. and Walker W. 'Government policies towards industrial innovation', *Research Policy*, vol. 5, no. 1, 1976.

Rapp J., 'Inventory management for small business', *Journal of Accountancy*, vol. 48, Feb., 1978.

Reuss G. E., 'Entrepreneurship in the area of management', In Bonaparte T. H. and Glaherty J. E. ed., *Peter Drucker, Contributions to Business Enterprise*, New York University Press, 1970.

Richards B., 'Improving small company performance: how the expert outsider can help', *Director*, vol. 33, no. 2, 1980.

Riggs C., 'The rise of women entrepreneurs', *Dun & Bradstreet Reports*, Jan./Feb., pp. 19–23, 1981.

Ritchie D. Asch D. and Weir A., 'The provision of assistance to small firms', *International Small Business Journal*, vol. 3, no. 1, 1984.

Robinson R., 'The importance of 'outsiders' in small firm /strategic planning', *Academy of Management Journal*, vol. 1, pp. 80–93, 1982.

Robinson R. B., 'Measures of small firm effectiveness for strategic planning research', *Journal of Small Business Management*, vol. 21, no. 2, pp. 22–9, 1983.

Said K. E. and Hughet J. K., 'Managerial problems of the small firm', *Journal of Small Business Management*, vol. 15, no. 1, 1977.

Scase R. and Goffee R., 'Why some women decide to become their own boss', *New Society*, vol. 61, no. 1034, 1982.

Scharz F. C., 'Value analysis for small businesses', *Journal of Small Business Management*, Vol. 12, no. 2, 1974.

Schreier J., 'Is the female entrepreneur different?', *MBA*, March, pp. 40–43, 1976.

Schwartz E., 'Entrepreneurship: a new female frontier', *Journal of Contemporary Business*, winter, 1976.

Sharma S. and Mahajan V., 'Early warning indicators of business failure', *Journal of Marketing*, vol. 44, autumn, pp. 80–89, 1980.

Smith A. D., 'Small retailers: prospects and policies', Committee of Inquiry on Small Firms, Research Report No. 15, London, HMSO, 1971.

Stanworth J. and Curran J., 'Growth and the small firm: an alternative view', *Journal of Management Studies*, vol. 13, no. 2, 1976.

Star A. D. and Massell M. Z., 'Survival rates for retailers', *Journal of Retailing*, vol. 57, no. 2, 1981.

Stone J. E., 'Survival for the small business owner', *National Public Accountant*, vol. 23, no. 6, 1978.

Storey D. J., 'Small firms: do they get too much advice?', *Bankers Magazine (London)*, vol. 224, March, 1981.

Vozikis G. and Glueck W. F., 'Small business problems and stages of development', *Academy of Management Proceedings*, 1980.

Watkins J. and Watkins D., 'The female entrepreneur', *International Small Business Journal*, vol. 2, no. 4, 1984.

Webster F. A., 'Entrepreneurs and ventures: an attempt at classification and clarification', *Academy of Management Review*, no. 2, pp. 54–63, 1977.

Wheelwright S. C., 'Strategic planning in the small business', *Business Horizons*, vol, 14, Aug., 1971.

Williams A. J., 'Why so many small businesses fail', *Real Estate Journal*, April, 1975.

Wilson Report, 'Financing small firms' (Interim report of the Committee to Review the Functioning of the Financial Institutions), HMSO, London, 1979, Cmnd 7503.

Wood E. G., 'How management can help small firms', *Management Consultant*, vol. 70, no, 5, 1978.

Books

Bannock G., *The Smaller Business in Britain and Germany*, Wilton House, London, 1976.

Bannock G., *The Organisation of Public Sector Promotion of Small Business*, Economists Advisory Group, London, 1980.

Bannock G., *Promoting the Small Business: An International Survey*, Croom Helm, London, 1981.

Bannock G., *The Economics of Small Firms*, Blackwell, Oxford, 1981.

Bates J., *The Financing of Small Business*, 3rd edn, Sweet & Maxwell, London, 1982.

Baumback C., Lawyer K. and Kelly P., *How to Organise Small Business*, Prentice Hall, Englewood Cliffs, NJ, 1968.

Bellamy C. and Child G. D., *Common Market Law of Competition*, Sweet & Maxwell, London, 1978.

Birch D. C., *The Job Generation Process*, (MIT Program on Neighbourhood and Regional Change), MIT, Cambridge, Mass., 1979.

Birley S., *New Enterprises: A Start-up Casebook*, Croom Helm, London, 1982.

Blackburn A. C., *Consultancy for Small Firms*, Brunel University School of Social Studies, 1969.

Boswell J., *The Rise and Decline of Small Firms*, Allen & Unwin, London, 1973.

Brockhause R., *The Psychology of the Entrepreneur*, In Kent C. et al. eds, *Encyclopaedia of Entrepreneurship*, Prentice Hall, Englewood Cliffs, NJ, 1982.

Brooks A., *Black Businesses in Lambeth*, Directorate of Town Planning, London Borough of Lambeth, 1982.

Brown C. E., *Management Problems of a Small Firm*, Imperial College of Science and Technology, London, 1977.

Bruckey S. W. ed., *Small Business in American Life*, Columbia University Press, New York, 1980.

Confederation of British Industry, *Small Firms in the Economy*, CBI, London, 1981.

Campbell A., *Worker Owners: The Mondragon Achievement*, Anglo-German Foundation, London, 1977.

Clarke P., *Small Businesses: How They Survive and Succeed*, David & Charles, Newton Abbot, 1972.

Clarke P., *Political Economy of Co-operation*, Oxford University Press, Oxford, 1980.

Collins O. and Moore D. G., *The Enterprising Man*, Michigan State University, Michigan, 1964.

Danco L. A., *Inside the Family Business*, Centre for Family Businesses, Cleveland, Ohio, 1976.

Dawson J. A. and Kirby D. A., *Small Scale Retailing in the UK*, Saxon House, London, 1979.

Day W. H., *Maximising Small Business Profits with Precision Management*, Prentice Hall, Englewood Cliffs, NJ, 1978.

Deeks J., *The Small Firm Owner-Manager*, Praeger, New York, 1976.

Department of Industry/Shell UK, *Helping Small Firms Start Up and Grow: Common Services and Technological Support*, HMSO, London, 1982.

Dewhurst J. and Burns P., *Small Business Finance and Control*, Macmillan, Basingstoke, 1984.

Doyle W. J., *A Survey of the Services Available to Assist Small UK Firms in Export Marketing*, City University Business School, London, 1977.

Economic and Social Committee, *The Situation of Small and Medium-sized Undertakings in the European Community*, EEC, Brussels, 1975.

Economists Advisory Group, *Small Firms and Employment*, Smaller Businesses Association, London, 1974.

Farrell P., *How to Buy a Business*, Kogan Page, London, 1983.

Fothergill S. and Gudgin G., *The Job Generation Process in Britain*, Centre for Environmental Studies, London, 1979.

Gibb A. and Webb T., *Policy Issues in Small Business Research*, Saxon House, London, 1980.

Golzen L., *Taking up a Franchise*, Kogan Page, London, 1983.

Gorb P., Dowell P. and Wilson P., *Small Business Perspectives*, Armstrong, London, 1981.

Hamilton R. T., *Government Decisions in Small Firms, Government and Industry*, Open University, Milton Keynes, 1976.

Harper M, *Consultancy for Small Businesses*, Intermediate Technology Publications, London, 1977.

Herbert A. S., *Reason in Human Affairs*, Blackwell, Oxford, 1983.

Hertz L., *In Search of a Small Business Definition*, University Press of America, Lanham, 1981.

Johns B. L., Dunlop W. C. and Sheehan W. J., *Small Businesses in Australia: Problems and Prospects*, Allen & Unwin, London, 1978.

Jones C. D., *Consultancy in the Smaller Firm*, Department of Industry, London, 1974.

Jones J. and Parry W. H., *How to Start, Run, and Succeed in Your Own Business*, Wheatsheaf Books, Brighton, 1983.

Korah V., *Competition Law of Britain and the Common Market*, Elek Books, London, 1975.

Kotler P., *Principles of Marketing*, Prentice Hall, Englewood Cliffs, NJ, 1980.

Lace G., *Effective Marketing for the Smaller Business*, Scope, Newbury, 1983.

Lace G. *Government Aid for Small Business*, Institute of Chartered Accountants in England and Wales, London, 1980.

Levicki C. ed., *Small Business: Theory & Policy*, Croom Helm, London, 1984.

Light I. H., *Ethnic Enterprise in America*, University of California, Berkeley, Ca., 1972.

Liles P. R., *New Business Ventures and the Entrepreneur*, Irwin, Homewood, I., 1974.

Little A. D., *New Technology Based Small Firms in the UK and the Federal Republic of Germany*, Wilton House, London, 1977.

Lowe J. F. and Crawford N. K., *Technology Licensing and the Growing Firm*, Pergamon Press, Oxford, 1983.

McClelland D. C., *The Achieving Society*, Princetown, Van Nostrand, Wokingham, 1961.

McClelland D. C. and Winter D. G., *Motivating Economic Achievement*, Free Press, New York, 1969.

Mendelsohn M., *The Guide to Franchising*, Pergamon Press, Oxford, 1982.

Meredith G. G., *Small Business Management in Australia*, McGraw Hill, Sydney, 1982.

Moyer R. B. and Goldstein S., *The First Two Years: Problems of Small Firm Growth & Survival*, Small Business Administration, Washington, 1981.

OECD, *Innovation in Small and Medium Firms*, OECD, Paris, 1982.

Oakeshott R., *Case for Worker Co-operatives*, Routledge, London, 1978.

Odlin D., *Finding a Suitable Incentive for a Small Company*, London Business School, 1975.

Peterson R., *Small Business, Building and Balanced Economy*, Press Porcepic, Erin, Ontario, 1977.

Ray G. and Hutchinson P., *The Financing and Financial Control of Small Enterprise Development*, Gower, Epping, 1983.

Rothwell R. and Zegveld W., *Innovation and the Small and Medium Sized Firm*, Frances Pinter, London, 1982.

Scase R. and Goffee R., *The Real World of the Small Business Owner*, Croom Helm, London, 1980.

Schumacher F., *Small is Beautiful*, Blond & Briggs, London, 1973.

Shames W. H., *Venture Management*, Free Press, New York, 1974.

Smith N. R. *The Entrepreneur and His Firm: The relationship between the type of man and type of company*, Michingan State University Press, 1967.

Stanworth M. J. K. and Curran J., *Management Motivation in the Small Firm*, Gower, Epping, 1973.

Stevens M., *30 Small Business Mistakes and How to Avoid Them*, Prentice Hall, Englewood Cliffs, NJ, 1978.

Storey D.J., *Entrepreneurship and the New Firm*, Croom Helm, London, 1982.

Storey D. J., *Job Generation and Small Firms Policy in Britain*, Centre for Enviromental Studies, London, 1980.

Storey D. J. ed., *The Small Firm, An International Survey*, Croom Helm, London, 1983.

Thornley J., *Workers Co-operatives: Jobs and Dreams*, Heinemann, London, 1981.

Vanek J., *Self-management*, Penguin, Harmondsworth, 1981.

Vaughan C. L., *Franchising: Its Nature and Scope*, Lexington Books, Lexington, Mass., 1979.

Watkins D., Stanworth I. and Webster A. eds., *Stimulating Small Firms*, Gower, Epping, 1982.

Wood E. G., *Bigger Profits for the Smaller Firm*, 2nd edn, Business Books, London, 1978.

Woodcock C., *Raising Finance*, Kogan Page, London, 1982.

Index